PRAISE GOD FOR TATTERED DREAMS

WHY DOES GOD LET BAD THINGS HAPPEN?

On the flipside, why does He let **good** things happen? Having been in conversation with God for several years, I believe He lets things—good and bad—happen because He created us with free will. Everything that happens on this planet is the end result of what people have been doing down here since the dawn of time.

God could be saving us from ourselves, but meddling in our affairs would be contrary to how He created us. God's guidance is, however, available to any saved person who asks for it. **PRAISE GOD FOR TATTERED DREAMS** describes how a near-fatal stroke prompted me to declare peace with God and start asking Him for direction.

Writing this book was invigorating, sorrowful, freeing, maddening, enlightening, and frightening. You'll probably feel these emotions, and others, as you read. You'll also experience what it's like to face the world each day with an acute brain injury. My prayer is that **PRAISE GOD FOR TATTERED DREAMS** may even prompt you to relinquish some control, and let God lead you home.

Suffering a near-fatal stroke at 33 wasn't on my to-do list but it did open my eyes to the reality I could choose to live forever. Like you, I don't know what the next moment holds but I do know my last step will lead me into God's presence for eternity. May you, too, live happily ever after.

THE FINE PRINT

PRAISE GOD FOR TATTERED DREAMS includes some medical information, which wasn't written by a doctor. If some of it piques your curiosity, you should discuss it with your doctor. Similarly, information about where God has led my thinking may be specific to me. You'll need to form your own relationship with God, through Jesus Christ, to see where He leads your thinking.

Published by http://www.Lulu.com/

First edition 2009

ISBN 978-0-578-03375-4

PRAISE GOD
FOR TATTERED
DREAMS

iv

CONTENTS

PREFACE

All names used in *Praise God for Tattered Dreams* are pseudonyms because any glory associated with this book should go directly to God. If you think you know the true identity of anyone mentioned, please keep it to yourself.

Bible verses included in *Praise God* come from the King James Version (KJV). If you choose to read a different version of the Bible, I suggest you compare the wording to that in the KJV on occasion.

This book is about MY stroke, not A stroke or THE stroke. I earned the privilege of claiming it as my own. Besides, adopting the word MY marked a huge step forward in my recovery.

As you know, when different people describe a situation, you'll hear as many different versions as there are people. Due to the severity of my stroke, parts of *Praise God* are based on what others have told me. If their individual account of a situation is different from mine, my bad.

If I use a word you've never seen before, please consult your favorite dictionary. If you can't find a definition there, my bad, again.

CHAPTER 1

STUMBLING AROUND
IN THE DARK

Have you ever wondered why you exist? Years ago, a dear friend of mine was struggling with the proverbial, "Why Am I Here?" question. I wasn't sure how to help Jay so I simply led him to a mirror and asked him what he saw. Chills ran down my spine when Jay said, "Nothing…I see nothing." Much to my surprise, I heard myself reply, "Well, God has a plan for you. All you need to do is figure out what it is."

God must have been speaking through me because that conversation took place almost 20 years before I realized Jesus Christ had died so I could stand before God as if I'd never sinned. The only thing I did to receive His Grace, was come to believe Jesus had died and been resurrected so I could choose to remove the stain of sin from my life.

This forgiveness is something I could never have earned, regardless of any good works or religious involvement I might pursue. Lack of knowledge is seldom enough to keep me quiet but I was certainly unprepared to talk about God back then.

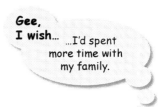

Gee, I wish… …I'd spent more time with my family.

1

My verbal abilities emerged early in life when I began talking before walking, the opposite of what most child development guides predict. That may have been the first medical anomaly in my life, but I've added more impressive ones.

Mom, a teacher, and Dad, an electrician, nurtured my innate communication skills throughout childhood. My older brothers, Ronald (Ron) and Victor (Vic), also fueled my desire to speak. Apparently, I realized early-on I could use words to get them to do things for me rather than having to do them myself. Although I was a few years away from learning the power of the pen, I learned as a toddler that words can motivate people to action.

It was Ron, four years my senior, who gave me a nickname along the lines of *Gabby Abby*, prompted by my incessant talking. He hasn't used that nickname since I was about ten but I recalled it recently. It fascinates me how I often struggle to remember what happened minutes ago, while vividly recalling memories from decades ago (more about *why* later).

These long-term memories resurface periodically in what I call *blasts from the past*. These *blasts* usually surface in my sleep, leading me to awaken with some bizarre notion on my mind. Searching my memory to find the source of these remembrances strikes me as good brain exercise, and quality entertainment. Those mentioned in this book are shown in shaded text to indicate an interruption in the narrative flow.

My brothers and I grew-up in a setting today's youth might consider ideal, albeit unusual. We lived with both of our parents in a century-old, two-story farmhouse on ten acres of land in the Midwest. Our acreage provided abundant outdoor activities and wholesome responsibilities. My brothers and I tended the *livestock*, generally a dog, several cats, and a pony, year-round. We also helped Mom and Dad plant, tend, and harvest a few acres of vegetables each summer. Mom canned, froze, or stored most of the veggies; Ron, Vic, and I sold the balance to *city folks*.

My brothers and I also earned a decent income through the ultimate newspaper business. We grew-up about 12 miles from three small cities, each of which had a weekly newspaper for local residents. All three papers were printed on the same day, and

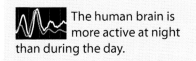
The human brain is more active at night than during the day.

Ron realized we could complete—and be paid-for—three routes by making one trip around town each week.

After school on Thursday, we'd stuff a copy of each paper in a small, plastic sack and then deliver them in one fell swoop. Depending on the weather, we three would ride our bikes, pull our sleds, or beg Mom to drive us around town. Regardless of how we traveled, Dad required me to always be with at least one other family member. He was very protective of me, throughout my childhood.

> One time, I got ticked at Ron while stuffing the sacks and tossed one from the previous week into his pile. The recipient noticed and was none too happy. Sorry about that, Ron.

If you're thinking I spent a lot of time with my brothers and our mom, you're right. As a teacher, Mom worked the same hours as we did as students, and was home with us each summer break. We also spent a lot time with Dad. Although he worked full-time, Dad was home by 4:30 every afternoon, without fail, and chose to spend his evenings tending our acreage, playing with us, and helping with homework.

The only time I recall our family being divided for a period of time was while Mom completed her graduate degree, attending class one night a week for a few months. It was so unusual for her to be gone in the evening, Dad let my brothers and me *camp-out* on the dining room floor on Mom's class nights. It made all four of us feel better to be in the same room when she was out and about. Dad made the most of these hours alone with us by reading Laura Ingalls Wilder's books about the American frontier aloud.

The quiet of my childhood seems like a distant memory these days. Although it was sometimes boring to live in the country, it was also easy to be still, and know that God is God (Psalms 46:10). I was still separated from Him by sin back then but could somehow sense God's presence, and would occasionally have a one-sided conversation with Him. That verse is a cakewalk for me now, except for the "Be still" part. As this world gets busier, louder, and more dangerous, it gets more and more challenging to find a time and place conducive to feeling God's presence. Perhaps that's why I protect my weekly worship celebrations (AKA church time) so carefully. Somehow, I'm able to tune-out the distractions of this world when I'm within the walls of God's house.

Our acreage kept my brothers and me fairly well-sequestered from the world, and the absence of a phone provided even more insulation until the mid 1970s. We could've afforded a phone long before then but Dad didn't see much point in having one, preferring instead to communicate face-to-face or through a personal letter. Only after repeated pleas from the local elementary principal, did Dad agree to a phone. Mom was a substitute teacher back then and the principal had grown tired of driving to our home to see if she was available to teach.

Dad finally relented—with some conditions. Our number would be unlisted and my brothers and I were expected to keep it private. We were also expected only to answer the phone and hand it to Mom or Dad. We weren't supposed to call our friends and, since they didn't know our number, they didn't call us. Apparently, Mom and Dad still expected **us** to communicate with people face-to-face when possible. Let me tell you, our mustard yellow, rotary phone was quite the piece of modern technology.

If you're thinking my dad sounds like a grumpy, old codger, let me assure you he has a truly kind heart, well-disguised by a slender, 6'9" frame, topped by a head kept perpetually shaved. Not that Dad has anything against a full head of hair; it's just that my brothers and I inherited our curly locks from him. Dad, Ron, and Vic seem to think curly hair looks okay on females but not males. As a result, they've opted to keep their hair very short or shorn for years. When Vic was in 4th grade, however, he decided he'd look cool with long hair and *forgot* to visit the barber shop for several weeks. At last, Dad invited him to step outside one Saturday morning and (unceremoniously) shaved him bald.

In contrast, Dad expected me to wear my hair long and forbid me to get a hair cut until I was 18. My mom did *give me* bangs when I was in junior high but the rest of my hair remained long until I started college. Dad also set an 18-year minimum on my staying overnight with friends, dating, and getting my ears pierced. Those rules were about as cool back then as they'd be today.

> In addition to my Dad-imposed social limitations, I was taller and more outspoken than the average girl. He gets the credit for both my height and penchant for candor. I recall Dad helping me accept the reality of my height by saying, "A tall girl hunched over doesn't look like a short girl. She looks like a tall girl hunched over."

Although Mom and Dad are both painfully frugal, I'm pretty sure it was Dad who decided I should wear my brothers' hand-me-downs, when possible. He did have a point; Ron's plaid, knit pants, and other *male* hand-me-downs fit me just fine. When you consider the whole package, let's just say I got teased a lot.

Fortunately, I entered this world with the gift of positive self-talk. The supportive feedback I've been giving myself since birth has helped me weather many storms, including childhood teasing and a massive stroke, as a young adult. Some people may not hear or recognize the feedback their brain provides. Worse yet, others may hear mostly negative feedback.

Positive self-talk was a *standard issue* for me, and it took years for me to realize that's what helps me overcome challenges others find daunting. Without the non-stop, encouraging monologue produced by—and for—my brain, my life probably would have ended years ago. I now know this constructive banter emanates from the Holy Spirit, because I began to distinctly recognize His promptings (AKA positive self-talk) after being saved.

If you don't hear or recognize the feedback your brain provides itself, or your brain provides mostly negative feedback, take heart. You have the rest of your life to retrain it. The first step is for you to get reconnected with God by removing the stain of sin from your life. There's no time like **now** to make that move. Feel free to read the *Epilogue* now, if you like. Just be sure to return to this page after reading it.

I think of a person's soul as the breath of God, which is present in him before he's even born. This breath is mentioned in Genesis 2:7, which says, "And the LORD God formed man of the dust of the ground, and breathed into his nostrils the breath of life; and man became a living soul." Besides, Genesis 1:26 tells us, "…God said, Let us make man in our image, after our likeness." The apple doesn't fall far from the tree, you know, even when the tree is unseen.

The Bible also says, in Romans 5:5, "…the love of God is shed abroad in our hearts by the Holy Ghost which is given unto us." This verse tells me that when a person acknowledges Jesus Christ died, was buried, and rose again so God would forgive his sins, his soul will be cleansed and he'll finally feel complete. I picture the breath mentioned above bursting into a gale-force wind when a person reaches this realization.

Believing the breath of God is in each person, even before birth, helps me understand why most children are drawn toward independence from a young age. It also helps me see why people sometimes survive life-threatening medical events. Surely, God's breath could provide the energy needed to pull a person's mind, body, and soul through trying times.

Easy, welcome times in my life don't push me to find God in the moment but challenging, unsettling times encourage me to stay in constant conversation with Him. I now know the primary reason for my existence is to glorify God and be in fellowship with Him. It's the *hard* times that provide opportunities for me to glorify God, and remind me His plan will come to fruition when this world ends. That realization prompted me to adopt, "Things always work out," as my life *philosophy* a few years post-stroke.

That simple statement reminds me, and those who hear me say it, that God has a plan for each of us. It also prompts me to remember each thought, word, and action I produce should glorify Him. The introductory chapter of First John provides an excellent summary of how those who follow God's plan for their life will be filled with joy in this earthly life before entering into eternal life with Him in Heaven. Consider 1 John 1:3 which says, "…truly our fellowship is with the Father, and with his Son Jesus Christ."

The situations I encounter in life do always work-out because God doesn't make mistakes. Every bump, fork, and curve in my life's road is part of His plan for me. Although He knows how my life will unfold, I'm in the driver's seat when it comes to what I make of each experience I encounter. Said another way, when I reach an unexpected jog in my life's road, I can choose to roll over and play dead, forge ahead as if I'm in-control, or follow God's guidance with each step I take.

I've never been one to roll over and play dead but I did spend the first 33 years of my life pretending I was in control of my life. In addition to being a born communicator, I'm an overachiever who enjoys tackling new challenges. My knack for communication blossomed in high school, where I relied on it to excel both in classes and extra-curricular activities. Would you believe the gift of gab can help a person through math, softball, band, and various other activities? Let's just say I can talk myself through anything.

My desire to be in control of my own life, prompted me to complete high school a semester early, and immediately start college. Like many freshmen, I didn't know what I wanted to be when I grew-up so I declared a major that interested me — psychology.

After realizing I'd probably need a Ph.D. to make a living in that field, I changed my major to business. One course in economics convinced me a business major would lead to an early, painful death. You see, I'm a right-brain kind of gal. Even as a child, I grasped what was occurring in complex situations, and used my language skills to help others understand what I saw. These cognitive skills reside primarily in the right hemisphere of the brain, which may explain why right-brain thinkers are sometimes called *big picture* thinkers. These folks usually prefer essay tests over multiple-choice ones and see most situations in shades of grey, rather than black-and-white.

The *other* (left) hemisphere approaches the world by looking at the parts in the big picture. Left-brain thinkers are often known as *detail* people. They tend to like multiple choice tests and typically view a situation as either black or white. There are a host of other differences between left- and right-brain thinkers, which are beyond the scope of this book.

The economics class mentioned above helped me realize most of my cognitive skills reside in my right hemisphere. With that reality in mind, I declared a major in English with a minor in philosophy. When I called my parents to share the news, Dad commended my decision to become a teacher like Mom. When I assured Dad I had no intention of teaching school, he whispered the news to Mom and handed her the phone. Mom proceeded to ask what kind of jobs there are for someone with a degree in English who doesn't want to teach. Without hesitation, I said, "I have no idea, Mom, but something will work out."

That wasn't typical of my conversations with Mom so I'm sure God was speaking through me again. And you know—He was right. Soon after declaring my new major, I met the man of my dreams, Troy, a statistics major who's as left-brain dominant as I am right-brain: the perfect match. About a year later, I accepted a technical writing internship with a seed company. After writing computer documentation there for a few months, I returned to college for my final semester.

That company offered me a full-time job as a technical writer between then and graduation day, so I spent my 22nd birthday (the day after graduation), packing my dorm room and moving into my first apartment. There was a lot to do that day because my job started the following day. Over the ensuing seven years, I married Troy, earned a master's degree in journalism/mass communications, bought a home, and brought our sons, Trent and Donald (Don), into this world.

Both Troy and I worked for the businesses we'd joined as college interns during this time. With my eyes on a flourishing career, I moved into the company's communications department in 1992. No matter where I went or what I did, I was in a hurry—focused on overachieving and keeping my life crammed full, 24/7. By the time my employer merged with another company in 1999, I was managing that group of communicators.

My impromptu approach to life seemed to be working pretty well, given my accomplishments by age 33. I was flying high and thought I had it all. My goals were aggressive and I was never happy to simply meet them. I led those around me to expect peak performance from me at all times. Simply meeting their expectations wasn't good enough; I chose to over-promise **and** over-deliver. My focus on materialistic goals kept me too busy to ask myself, "Why am I here?" Likewise, I didn't take time to ask God to share His opinion, let alone to listen for His answer.

My worldly successes did wonders for my self-confidence. I enjoyed regular opportunities to test and 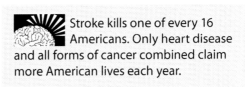 Stroke kills one of every 16 Americans. Only heart disease and all forms of cancer combined claim more American lives each year.

strengthen my communication skills at work, and as a wife and a mom. Although I didn't know where I was going or how I was going to get there, I sure was in a big hurry to accomplish *something*. It's no mystery I didn't know where I was bound; I hadn't asked our Creator about His plans for me. Perhaps that's why I spent 33 years trying to control my own destiny. During that time, I focused on exceeding my own expectations and those of people who seemed to know me well. My goals were set on what I expected of myself and what others expected of me.

It may have looked like I *had it all* pre-stroke, but there was an aching emptiness in my life. It's obvious to me now this void was the result of me being disconnected from God by sin. Romans 1:20 says, "For the invisible things of him from the creation of the world are clearly seen, being understood by the things that are made, even his eternal power and Godhead; so that they are without excuse."

This verse tells me that humans somehow sense God's presence and there's no good reason for anyone to live separated from Him by sin. Like many people, I did my best to fill that aching void with higher education, career success, family, material goods, friends, and general busyness. Now that I'm saved, I'll never feel empty or be lonely again.

One way I remind myself I'm not alone is by staying in constant conversation with God. My prayers were a one-sided conversation before I accepted Jesus Christ as my Lord and Savior. They were few and far between back then and often involved something I demanded in a crisis. It took years for me to realize God isn't a vending machine or magician; He's not waiting around to hear what I ask for so He can *magically* make it appear. However, now that God's Holy Spirit lives in me, my prayers are always answered. Better yet, they're answered so that I get what I need, even if that's not what I asked for (*AKA* want).

As Romans 8:26 says, "Likewise the Spirit also helpeth our infirmities: for we know not what we should pray for as we ought: but the Spirit itself maketh intercession for us with groanings which cannot be uttered." This verse tells me God's Holy Spirit lets Him know what I need even when I don't yet know I need it. This *direct line* to God is critical because a saved person ought to strive to fulfill our Creator's plan for his life. Life can be challenging even when we have clearly defined goals and action steps but at least the Holy Spirit gives us access to that information.

Of course, there are times when I'd rather talk with someone I can see. That's when it's great to know I now have family members around the world and nothing, even death, can separate me from them. That's because every saved person has one key element in common; we're walking through this life with the light of Jesus Christ in our heart. No matter where I go, I'm never far from another true Christian. Although I can't always pick a saved person out of a crowd, I know millions of people have accepted Christ's priceless gift. That reality makes life in this crazy world bearable.

It's wonderful to be free of all the stress and worries I used to cart-around. Words cannot explain how wonderful this freedom feels but I'm guessing the knights of old might liken it to the freedom they felt after removing their suit of armor. John 10:10 tells us, Jesus came to give us *abundant life*. My life with Jesus Christ enables me to relax when the going gets tough, make wise decisions, feel less anxious, and find joy in every situation.

By following in Jesus' footsteps, I can also overcome every temptation Satan casts my way. Since love for Christ overtook my life, I live for Him, not myself. By simply accepting the truth of His sacrifice, I was permanently freed from the bondage of any sin I'd ever committed or might commit in the future. It's so amazing to be completely free when I awaken each morning; the weight of the world is no longer on my shoulders. As an added bonus, I have no fear of death. Not that I'm in any hurry to reach that milestone, but surveys show ten out of ten people are mortal, so why sweat the details? Now that I'm just one step away from Glory — eternity with God in Heaven — it's all good.

The job I held pre-stroke often required me to meet with vice presidents and technical experts within the company to discuss pending business changes. Many times, these meetings focused on heated topics, lasted for hours, and included information I'd need to develop an effective communication plan. My questions and input generally helped these leaders see how typical employees might respond to a proposed change. Back then, I provided input with tact and diplomacy. My ability to accurately and immediately read how those gathered in the room were responding to my comments provided a way for me to shine.

It may have seemed everything was going my way but what I lacked was a clear understanding of what it means to *have it all*. The time and talents I invested in my various roles earned me plenty of tangible rewards, but I still had that aching emptiness. As I now see it, each person is born with a comparable feeling of disconnectedness because all humans are separated from God at their birth, by their desire to sin.

Only God's Holy Spirit can completely, permanently fill that void, and that happens only when a person accepts Jesus Christ as his personal Lord and Savior. Satan does his best to keep people from making that move because once a person is saved, he has a *reserved* spot in Heaven. Satan can't pull a saved person's soul back to his side but he still tempts that person to think, speak, and behave in ungodly ways. I think Satan does that because getting a saved person to succumb to temptation may push those who aren't yet saved, further away from God if they see his *fall*.

After all, if a Christian treats others badly, who'd want to follow in his footsteps? The only sinless person to ever live is our Lord and Savior, Jesus Christ. God tells us in Romans 3:23, "For all have sinned, and come short of the glory of God." It can be tough to get an unsaved person interested in learning about someone who sacrificed His Life for our good more than 2,000 years ago, but frighteningly easy for a Christian to get an unsaved person's attention by committing a sin.

Maintaining a personal relationship with Jesus Christ is the only way a person can feel completely whole. Jay, the friend mentioned earlier, calls this fix the *Jesus Piece*. In other words, the piece needed to fill the empty void in an unsaved person's life is exactly the size and shape of Jesus.

Perhaps the attention I gave my career explains why it took so long for me to realize my *Jesus Piece* was missing. After all, it certainly isn't because I was unaware of God's presence. My parents had insisted Ron, Vic, and I go to Sunday School every week from the age of about three. That's where I first learned how God became flesh and walked among us in the person of Jesus Christ for about 30 years. I also learned how Jesus Christ, our Lord and Savior, sacrificed His life to pave the way for all people to be in fellowship with God when He died for the forgiveness of our sins. Jesus' selfless sacrifice gives each person the option to cleanse his soul of sin and get reconnected with God.

Anyone can become a Christian, by simply confessing he's a sinner and acknowledging Jesus Christ died in his place so his sins would be forgiven. There aren't any strings attached to this deal, but you do need to accept Jesus' gift before you die. After taking this leap of faith, I suspect you'll feel drawn to invest your remaining days bringing glory to God and recruiting new and better disciples of Jesus Christ.

When I accepted Jesus' sacrifice, the Holy Spirit overtook my body and became available for non-stop conversation. 1 Corinthians 6:19-20 tell us, "What? Know ye not that your body is the temple of the Holy Ghost which is in you, which ye have of God, and ye are not your own? For ye are bought with a price: therefore glorify God in your body, and in your spirit, which are God's." These verses tell me that as a saved person journeying through life with God, I should take good care of myself.

Now that I'm walking through this life with Him, I know the only goal I <u>needed</u> in life was to ensure my soul will spend eternity with God when I die. That goal can only be **accepted**, not earned or achieved, yet somehow it took almost 40 years for me to reach it. The only requirement was to accept that Jesus Christ died in my place so my sins would be forgiven. His saving Grace is available to you, too, because Jesus' sacrificial death atones for the sins of all people. Jesus willingly gave His life so that anyone who accepts His gift would join God in Heaven after they die.

Hopefully, you realized, or will realize, at a younger age than me, that Jesus Christ was born, died, and rose again so God would forgive your sins (1 Corinthians 15:1-4). God and I weren't on speaking terms the first 30+ years of my life but somehow I knew He was there next to me. My responsibilities as a wife, mom, sister, daughter, aunt, employee, friend, etc. left me with no time or energy for anything else, including time to figure out what God has planned for me. What a blessing God loves me so much He waited patiently to get my attention, which happened when the distractions in my life were suspended by a massive stroke.

Many people view overachieving as a positive, but I now recognize it as a temptation, something that provides only temporary relief from feeling incomplete. At least I avoided obviously harmful patches, such as alcohol and drugs, which further erode a person rather than helping him feel whole. However, that emptiness haunted me, no matter what I achieved before I was saved. I think every unsaved person has a similar, aching emptiness in his heart.

Now I know it wouldn't have mattered how much I achieved, I would have felt incomplete until I realized Jesus Christ died, was buried, and rose again so God would forgive me of my sins. (I Corinthians 15:1-4). The only way anyone can feel truly whole is to relinquish control over his life and start a relationship with an invisible Being. Information about taking that leap of faith is included in the *Epilogue*. If you're one of the many people who have yet to take that leap of faith, I pray you'll take it before your final heartbeat. The reality of the situation is that you could die at any time. If you're still disconnected from God by sin when you die, your soul will spend eternity in hell—separated from God.

Since accepting Jesus' sacrifice, I feel complete because God's Holy Spirit inhabits my very being. Getting reconnected with God helped me realize the end of the road—death—is just a bump in the road between here and eternal life in Heaven. Fellowship with God also makes my life here on Earth joyful. Now that I'm in constant conversation with Him, I can find God's glory in every experience. Some day, I may face circumstances more horrific than my stroke and it's incredibly freeing to know those trials will only help me to proclaim God's glory in new and better ways.

My stroke dropped me to a fork in my life's road, a fork I might have reached on my own if I'd been paying attention to God. But no… I was too busy for Him. Besides, it was challenging in those days for anyone to get my attention, let alone impact my thinking. All circuits were busy.

There was no eternal value in what I accomplished before I was saved but now that I'm in constant conversation with God, I invest my spiritual gifts glorifying Him. When you take that leap of faith, you, too, may feel drawn to serve Him.

If you're still stumblin' around in your own darkness, trying to figure out who you are and what you want to be when you *grow-up*, consider this:

- God is the only One with access to the master plan of life, the big picture.
- Your life is one tiny piece of that picture, and God's the only One Who knows what role your piece plays.
- If you've never asked God what role He plans for your piece to fill, you can't possibly know why you're here. After all, how can you move forward with purpose until you have your Creator's insight?
- You can only expect an answer from God after you've re-established your connection with Him. That connection was broken by sin way back in the Garden of Eden.

- The only way to wipe the stain of sin from your life is
  to accept the sacrifice Jesus Christ made on the cross for
  all people, as described in the *Epilogue*.

Hee-Haw was one of the few TV shows my brothers and I
were allowed to watch when we were kids. My most memorable
blast from the past to date is the phrase BR549. When I
finally figured out where BR549 came from, I called Dad to
see if I was right. After he confirmed BR549 was the phone
number Junior Samples had for his used car lot on *Hee-Haw*,
I thanked him and hung-up.

Grandpa Jones, the delightful
banjo player on *Hee-Haw*, died
from complications of a stroke at 84.
My stroke occurred on what would have
been his 86th birthday.

CHAPTER 2

GREAT STROKES FELL LITTLE OAKS

Why learn about stroke? The only prerequisite for suffering a stroke is having a brain. Given that you can read, you're obviously qualified. You may have heard some information about stroke before but if you didn't know you're at risk, you probably weren't listening. Now you know, so please read on; this chapter might just save your life.

You know the drill: exercise regularly, abandon self-destructive habits, buckle-up, eat healthy foods, wear a helmet, and protect yourself from disease. There's no magic pill to make you immortal, or even healthy, but these habits will probably enhance and extend your stay here on Earth. As a saved person, one reason I now follow these habits is because my body is a temple of the Holy Spirit, which makes unhealthy behaviors sound like an insult to God.

Although I adopted most of these habits years before I was saved, I now take them much more seriously. After all, God sent His only Son to die in my place. One way I can

Gee, I wish... ...I'd known the warning signs of stroke.

show my gratitude is by keeping myself as healthy as possible so His Holy Spirit can keep shining through me. The one habit mentioned above which I hadn't fully adopted before being saved, was protecting myself from some common diseases, such as stroke.

Things have gotten pretty crazy in our sin-sick world so you'll need to take an active role in caring for your *temple*. Each of us is mortal but some causes of death are better understood and more avoidable than others. Although stroke can affect anyone at any time, it's often overlooked or misunderstood.

Neurological connections make me think of domino art. The artist omits a few dominoes so that if an accidental topple occurs, only a portion of the picture falls. These missing links must be added to create an effective topple. Similarly, if a few of someone's brain cells are missing, a thought can't topple freely through her brain.

Pre-stroke, I knew about protecting myself from high-profile diseases such as heart disease and even knew a bit about certain types of cancer. I knew next to nothing about stroke, however, until I learned about it through personal experience. Before I became a stroke survivor, I mistakenly thought stroke leaves a person at least partially paralyzed, challenges her ability speak, and leaves her a bit *dull* mentally. A girl in my high school had had a stroke at 16 so at least I knew stroke can affect a person at any age.

Although I've always been a bit of a hypochondriac, I missed out on learning the warning signs of stroke until after I had one. These warning signs, shown below, are distinctive and easy-to-memorize. Knowing the warning signs may benefit you or someone you love because someone in America has a stroke about every 45 seconds. Keep in mind, you can't judge a person's risk of stroke based on age because more than 1/3 of strokes affect people under age 60; about 20 percent of strokes strike someone under age 40.

If the prevalence of stroke isn't enough to scare you, consider the fact about 150,000 Americans die of stroke each year. Comparable statistics in other developed nations are equally chilling, making stroke the #3 cause of death and leading cause of long-term disability in developed countries worldwide.

Stroke Warning Signs

Please note that each stroke warning sign begins with the word **sudden**. A stroke occurs when something **suddenly** goes wrong in the brain.

1. Sudden confusion, trouble speaking or understanding
2. Sudden numbness or weakness of the face, arm or leg, especially on one side of the body
3. Sudden trouble seeing in one or both eyes
4. Sudden trouble walking, dizziness, loss of balance or coordination
5. Sudden, severe headache with no known cause

Call 911

If you experience one or more of these warning signs, or observe them in someone else, contact your local Emergency Response Service immediately. Time lost equals brain cells lost when someone has a stroke.

Benjamin Franklin prompted me to think of this chapter title with his, "Little strokes fell great oaks," saying. His wisdom tells me that taking small steps can lead to accomplishing significant tasks. Although Franklin's quote is probably referring to the strokes of an axe, it also applies to the type of strokes doctors often call cerebral vascular accidents or brain attacks. A stroke that damages or kills *only* a few brain cells permanently changes the stroke survivor's life. These changes may be subtle or distinct but they do exist.

This means that if I apply Franklin's saying to the disease called stroke, a little stroke could fell a great oak (AKA strapping human). Thankfully, medical experts now know what factors increase a person's stroke risk, know how to mitigate many of those risks, and have devised some life-saving treatment options. For those fortunate enough to survive a stroke, new therapy options are regularly identified to help them recover.

The medical advances made since Franklin's days have yet to make a dent in stroke statistics, however. Perhaps that's because most people think stroke won't happen to them. Many people seem more comfortable accepting the fact they're at risk of having a heart attack than of having a stroke. Perhaps that's because the heart is a fairly standard-issue organ whereas the brain is so personal.

Maybe it's just less alarming to learn that a hunk of muscle you were born with may get hurt than it is to find-out the brain cells you've been carefully cultivating since birth through education and experience can get injured. Besides, the thinking abilities controlled by our brain define who we are. When a person's brain gets injured, so does her identify.

To me, living with the deficits of stroke is like losing a few pieces of a favorite, 2,000-piece jigsaw puzzle. I can still **almost** put the puzzle together but when I'm done, the picture's not quite right. Worse yet, I see the same incomplete picture and keep searching for missing pieces every day. These missing pieces are the brain cells killed by my stroke.

STROKE 101

Stroke is a cardiovascular disease affecting the arteries leading to and within the brain. A stroke occurs when blood, which carries oxygen and nutrients, can't reach all areas of the brain. When that happens, the oxygen-deprived cells start to die. This restriction in blood flow can happen when an artery is blocked or ruptures.

Blocked arteries account for more than 80 percent of all strokes. These *ischemic* strokes are usually caused by a blood clot, which either forms in the brain or travels there from another part of the body. Having an *ischemic* stroke is kind of like having a frozen pipe in your plumbing system.

> More than 80 percent of strokes are caused by restricted blood flow to the brain, often caused by a blood clot. Less than 20 percent of strokes are caused by a brain hemorrhage. Hemorrhagic, or massive, strokes are fatal far more often than ischemic strokes.

When that happens, water can't reach the faucets, toilets, or appliances (dishwasher, refrigerator, washing machine, etc.) that pipe usually *feeds*. Losing these services is a major nuisance but, if you're lucky, the fix is simple and inexpensive.

With an ischemic stroke, brain cells which normally receive oxygen-rich blood from the blocked vessel die because the vessel responsible for feeding them *freezes*. Losing any of your brain's abilities is a major problem and no amount of money can buy a fix. If you have a parent, sibling, or child who's had an ischemic stroke, you have an increased risk of stroke so be sure your primary care physician is aware of that history.

The remaining 20 percent of strokes are caused by a hemorrhage inside the skull. This type of stroke is caused when a blood vessel in the brain bursts, flooding the area around the rupture, splattering blood on brain cells here and there, and shutting down the flow of blood to areas of the brain previously served by that vessel.

This type of stroke is comparable to having the water main in your home burst, which causes a huge rush of water and a flooded basement. As a result, you have the problem mentioned above to contend with and lots of water to clean-up. At first glance you may only see that a foot of water is standing in the lower level of your home. Suddenly, you realize all this water in the basement also means no water is available to feed the pipes going to various rooms throughout your home. Not only is the water drowning valued items, it's also depriving your family of the water needed to complete basic, everyday tasks.

Get the picture? Restricting blood flow to one area of the brain is bad. Restricting blood flow to an area of the brain while simultaneously drowning other areas is **way** bad. In addition to being fatal more often than ischemic strokes, hemorrhagic strokes also tend to damage the brain more severely and in disparate areas. That's because brain cells, like all cells in our body, need a consistent supply of oxygen to survive. This oxygen is supplied by our blood. Sound like a good reason to keep your cardiovascular system working well?

You may have heard of another type of stroke called a transient ischemic attack, TIA, or mini-stroke. These differ from a full-blown stroke in that symptoms last less than a day and no brain cells actually die, they're just sort-of *on hold* for a while. A TIA is the ultimate warning sign you're at risk of having a major stroke.

The warning signs of stroke and TIA are identical and warrant immediate medical evaluation.

STROKE RISK FACTORS

This chapter opens with a back-handed compliment: you have a brain so you're qualified to have a stroke. Your actual risk of having a stroke is a combination of your family history, how you live, and your age. Each trait listed below increases a person's risk of stroke:

- **GENDER** Men account for more than half of all strokes but more women die of stroke than men.

- **RACE** Those of African descent have a higher stroke risk than others.

- **FAMILY HISTORY** If you have a parent, sibling, or child who had an ischemic stroke or TIA, your risk of stroke increases. Diseases such as diabetes, high blood pressure, heart disease, high cholesterol, carotid disease, atrial fibrillation, and sickle cell anemia may also increase your risk of stroke. If you inherited a disease that increases your risk of stroke, you can't change that fact, but you can follow your doctor's orders about carefully managing that disease.

- **HOW YOU LIVE** Choices you make about how you treat your body have an impact on your health and how long you'll live. Some less-than-healthy lifestyle choices may be tough to shake but it has to beat spending the rest of your life impaired by stroke. How well are you doing with the modifiable stroke risks listed below?

  - **SMOKING** This is the #1 modifiable stroke risk factor.

  - **POOR NUTRITION** Talk with your doctor about how saturated fat, trans fats, cholesterol, sodium, and calories impact stroke risk.

  - **LACK OF EXERCISE AND OBESITY** Try to get at least 30 minutes of physical activity each day. Inactivity and obesity each increase your risk of stroke.

  - **AGE** Your risk of stroke increases with age, and we all get older, up to a point.

Don't you just love how modifiable and non-modifiable risk factors are intertwined? They can introduce some not-so-nice challenges if they team-up against us. You really should consider addressing your modifiable risks, particularly if you have some non-modifiable ones working against you. More detailed information about stroke risk factors is provided on the American Stroke Association website at *http://www.strokeassociation.org.*

STROKE DEFICITS

The *collection* of **mis**information I had about stroke, prior to becoming a stroke survivor, included a stereotype of how stroke affects a person. It didn't take long for me to abandon my stereotype of stroke survivors once I realized it didn't apply to me. Stroke can interfere with any combination of physical and cognitive functions; it can even affect **all** functions. However, if communication between the brain and **all** body parts breaks down, there is no stroke survivor, there's a stroke victim.

The variety and severity of a survivor's deficits depend on the location and severity of her brain injury. An amazing assortment of stroke survivors has crossed my path since my stroke in January of 2000. Each one faces a unique set of challenges. Whenever I meet a stroke survivor for the first time, I must remind myself the brain is the only body part physically injured by stroke. Stroke can cause an amazing variety of deficits, only some of which are visible to others.

I've met stroke survivors living with:
- ability to utter only obscenities
- balance problems
- chronic pain
- disorientation
- fingers and/or toes that won't uncurl
- high distractibility
- immature social skills
- impaired problem-solving skills
- inability to: multitask, speak or understand spoken

words, swallow safely, understand humor and sarcasm,
write and read
- one side paralyzed, partially or completely
- poor judgment and awareness of safety threats
- psychological challenges such as depression, apathy,
  and paranoia
- vision challenges

Challenges such as these, as well as others I've only read about, prompted me to realize that although many people physically survive stroke, they're permanently changed by the experience. I know the person I was before my stroke is dead-and-gone. Fortunately, I have the rest of my life to discover the *new* me. I regularly remind myself of that as I go about adjusting to my new definition of *normal*. If you were to meet me on the street these days, I highly doubt you'd suspect I had a massive stroke.

You might notice my walk is a bit stilted or that I talk non-stop. You may even pick-up on the fact I have about as much tact as a 14-year-old. Trust me. These deficits were caused by stroke as surely as the stereotypical ones of paralysis and slurred speech which affect many survivors.

Those who knew me well before my stroke recognize the differences between the old me (died Jan. 30, 2000) and the new me (sprang to life Jan. 31, 2000). I'm almost the same physically but quite the new creation inside. Jesus Christ paved the way for my new self to emerge when He died on a cross more than 2,000 years ago. All it took was a good *boot to the head* for the Holy Spirit to get my attention.

It seems to me more bicyclists and motorcyclists are wearing helmets these days than in the past. Perhaps that means people are getting the message the human brain is very fragile. I hope this knowledge prompts you to take good care of your brain. Protecting your brain is critical because unlike the cells that make-up our skin, hair, and fingernails, when a brain cell dies, it's not replaced.

This reality strikes me as one way God displays His wonderful sense of humor. The most complex organ He created is also one of our most vulnerable. Not only that, God created the left hemisphere of our brain to control the right side of our body, and vice versa. The left side is also responsible for doing most analytical thinking, such as math and science, while the right side handles creative thoughts, such as singing, drawing, and writing.

> A teenage girl in my hometown had a stroke when I was in junior high. It seemed so mysterious for a young person's life to change so dramatically, and without any warning.

You could picture your brain's hemispheres as your body's co-captains. These hemispheres process information differently and specialize at different tasks. As is often the case, one co-captain probably dominates the other. Although you're inclined to process information in your dominant hemisphere, your best thinking comes when you get both sides working together.

An injury to any part of the brain will permanently alter a person's life, but one in the dominant hemisphere will have more impact than an injury on the *other* side. Given that my pre-stroke life was built on strong right-brain skills and tight connections between my hemispheres, the injury caused by my stroke prompted significant changes in my life.

Having a hemorrhage in my right hemisphere was bound to change my life because that's where most of the cognitive skills needed for clear, concise communication reside. Since I've never been particularly good at, or interested in math, the left hemisphere's forté, I don't think a few fried wires on that side would have rocked my world.

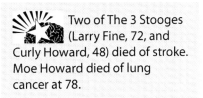
Two of The 3 Stooges (Larry Fine, 72, and Curly Howard, 48) died of stroke. Moe Howard died of lung cancer at 78.

CHAPTER 3

THE END OF
MY BEGINNING

Revelation 1:8 tells us "I am Alpha and Omega, the beginning and the ending, saith the Lord, which is, and which was, and which is to come, the Almighty."

This verse helps me grasp the breadth of eternity better than anything else I've read. When you consider how big eternity sounds in this verse, the span of a human life — birth to death — must be but a blip on God's radar screen. Even when a person lives to a ripe-old age, those years are brief in light of eternity's timeline.

One heartbeat ended the carefully planned life I built in my first 33 years. Chaos erupted inside my skull on Jan. 30, 2000, when my right middle cerebral artery, a major blood vessel near the center of the brain, burst. This hemorrhage prevented some brain cells from receiving the oxygen-rich blood they need to survive, while simultaneously drowning other cells. Each beat of my heart forced more blood through the broken vessel, causing a flood inside my skull.

That hemorrhage resulted in my having a massive stroke. My brain was suddenly challenged with surviving a

Gee, I wish… …I'd taken a hot air balloon ride.

massive flood while struggling to maintain contact with my body.
This busyness should explain why this chapter and the following
two are based on what a few trusted souls have told me rather than
my memory. As the saying goes, my mind was elsewhere.

Mom wrote the following in her journal:

Feb. 3
Dad up. We thought E wouldn't live. Relatives all there.
Marlene and Jeanne came. Many college and Troy and E's
friends. Many prayer chains. Toward evening some better.
We're told 10 to 20% chance of survival. We'd say squeeze
your hand. You could some with right hand, but not left. You
were paralyzed on left side.

How amazing my brain could keep me alive even after parts of
it had died and other parts are fighting to stay alive. The human
body surely must be, "fearfully and wonderfully made," as God
says in Psalms 139.

Life seemed to be going my way until that fateful moment. The
possibility of having a stroke had never even crossed my mind (pun
intended). In fact, I hadn't even completely accepted the fact that
I'm mortal, just like every other person. Given that death applies
to everyone, it seems reasonable for each of us to invest some time
considering where our soul will spend eternity when our earthly
body dies. Any time I'd spent planning for the future when I was
33 was focused on how much money we'd need for retirement,
though, not where my soul will spend eternity. That focus shifted
when my stroke made it painfully obvious I **will** die… someday.

> When Don was born, I had time to say one word to the
> doctor who delivered him. As he strode into my room, I said,
> "Catch!"

What a blessing God loves you and me, and knows each of us
better than we know ourselves. Psalms 139 is a wonderful reminder
of this truth. Verse 16 says, "Thine eyes did see my substance, yet

being unperfect; and in thy book all my members were written, which in continuance were fashioned, when as yet there was none of them."

I'd never entertained the possibility I was qualified to have a stroke back then. Being a parent provided plenty of *relevant* things to worry about. Ah… those were the days. The sheer bliss of not knowing the only prerequisite for having a stroke is having a brain. That simple fact makes stroke a potential threat for everyone. Although some people have a greater stroke risk than others, a brain attack — like a heart attack — can affect anyone, anywhere, at any time. That's why you should know the stroke warning signs mentioned earlier and be prepared to seek medical help immediately if you experience one or observe one in another person.

Although I've been a bit of a hypochondriac from an early age, my concerns about illness and death hadn't prompted me to learn about stroke in my first 33 years. That combination of ignorance about stroke and bliss about my life gave stroke the opportunity to make a sneak attack on my brain.

A sudden, severe headache (Warning Sign #5 mentioned earlier) hit me at work on Thursday, Jan. 27. However, with a 17-year history of migraine headaches, the cause of my throbbing head seemed obvious. Something must have seemed different about this headache though because a handful of colleagues later told me I'd described it as, "The worst migraine of my life."

Here's some perspective behind that statement. On a pain scale of one to ten, with one being pain-free and ten being excruciating, my average migraine was probably an eight. I'd rate childbirth, which I experienced twice, about a four. My pre-stroke headache must have been excruciating.

My head hurt so badly I called my husband, Troy, to let him know I wouldn't be much help at home that evening. Trent and Don were young enough at the time that keeping them corralled single-handedly took some advance warning. With that detail addressed, I made it through the day, probably with the help of the prescription painkillers I routinely took for migraines.

> **SideNote:** If you suffer from migraine headaches, I suggest you get your doctor's opinion of whether or not that increases your risk of stroke.

I called my mom that evening to tell her about my aching head. Somehow, I seem to feel better when Mom knows what's going on in my life. She probably wasn't too concerned because she'd witnessed many of my migraines.

I'm sure I got a fitful night's sleep before dragging myself to work on Friday. Most of my colleagues were accustomed to my two-day migraine cycle. Day 1 involved intense pain, visual disturbances, and strong medication. I used to call Day 2 my *headache hangover*. That sounds better than saying I felt like I'd been hit by a train, doesn't it? This Day 2 was different, however; the throbbing in my head hadn't abated.

Time used to stand still for me when I had a migraine, but I'd learned in my 17 years of experience that the world did keep moving. Although I'm now a big fan of listening to my body and responding to its cries for help, back then it seemed more important to maintain my frenetic pace. With those two forces at odds, I chose to keep numbing my pain and ventured into work on Jan. 28. It must have taken a lot of pain pills for me to make it through that day.

The illusion my headache was *only* a migraine continued into the weekend. Saturday, Jan. 29, was probably like most of our Saturdays back then—the four of us relaxing at home, entertaining our herd of cats: Mookie, Ping, and Puck. Mookie, my Valentine's gift to Troy in 1989, probably stayed with me constantly that day. She'd earned the nickname *Nurse Cat* soon after we adopted her because Mookie was pure white and had an uncanny ability to recognize when one of us wasn't feeling well—physically or emotionally. When her *nurse cat* radar went off, Mookie kept watch at her ailing human's side constantly.

Sundays in our home had been predictable for several years so I'm sure the boys and I went to Sunday School on Jan. 30, regardless of how I was feeling. Sunday morning remains my favorite time of the week because it offers activities which help set my heart and mind on how I can bring glory to God throughout the coming week.

This Sunday was a bit different, however, because it was Super Bowl Sunday. Troy decided to watch the game at home rather than going out with his friends. Since there isn't much to do outside in the Midwest in January, I called Mom after Sunday School to ask if the boys and I could go visit her and Dad. The note she jotted in her journal follows:

Jan. 30
E called saying she and the boys would be in town. I said no, too much snow here. The Rams won the Super Bowl.

As an alternative, I took the boys to a local mall to burn off some steam and to see *Stuart Little*, a movie they'd been wanting to see. My imagination won't even entertain what might have happened to our sons if I'd had my stroke while sitting in a crowded movie theater with them. Two precious boys, ages one and four, sitting with an unresponsive woman, surrounded by strangers... not good. If I'd had my stroke while driving to or from the mall, it's likely the three of us, and possibly others, would have died in an accident.

By the Grace of God, however, we arrived home safely after the movie. The four of us lounged around the living room during the Super Bowl until the boys went to bed. Troy then helped me to the bathroom because I'd apparently decided to get ready for bed, and try sleeping away the pain. He must have suspected something was seriously wrong, though, because he came into the bathroom to check on me a few minutes later. Troy says I'd fallen to the floor and couldn't talk or move.

He recalls talking to me and gently poking me until I opened my eyes briefly and said, "Call the paramedics." Those were the last words I spoke for about three days. My right middle cerebral artery, a key blood vessel near the middle of the brain, had ruptured and brain cells in various parts of my brain were being deprived of the oxygen-rich blood they need to survive.

Somehow, in my incredibly altered state of mind, just before my stroke, I put 2-and-2 together and told Troy what he needed to do. My brain reached the unnerving conclusion something was seriously wrong while having a near-fatal hemorrhage. Somehow I knew I needed help desperately, and some- one else would need to summon it for me.

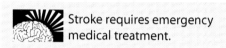 Stroke requires emergency medical treatment.

A very fuzzy recollection tells me I considered telling Troy to, "Call 9-1-1," but decided he might mistakenly think we needed the police. In a *normal* state of mind, I'm sure I would have said that instead of saying *paramedics*. Isn't the human mind a brilliant piece of work? Only God could create such as masterpiece.

Troy did as I said and called the paramedics. After providing the information needed for them to respond, he called his parents and asked them to come over. Troy assumed I'd be going to the hospital, and knew he'd need to be there to provide information on my behalf. With those calls for help completed, Troy faced an awkward dilemma. He wanted to notify my parents but didn't know their unlisted phone number. I didn't have it written down anywhere because I'd grown-up knowing it.

Troy thought to get their number from my brother, Vic. Unfortunately, it was about 10:30 p.m. on Vic's birthday. A phone call like the one Troy placed is never pleasant to receive, but particularly not on one's birthday. He told Vic what was going on, got my parents' number for future reference, and then asked him to call my folks.

I'm sure fear rushed through Mom's mind when she answered the phone that evening. From her perspective, any call that late in the day can't be good news. Mom says that when she recognized Vic's voice she was certain there'd been an accident. Of course, she was referring to an *auto* accident, not a *cerebral vascular* accident.

Troy's parents reached our home soon after he called Vic. My in-laws live about 20 miles from us but managed to get there before the local paramedics. Their quick response to Troy's call for help is typical of how supportive both of our families have been since that day. We are truly blessed to have so many relatives and friends who were willing to put their own lives on hold to help us through this difficult time.

If I experienced the bright light and overwhelming sense of bliss reported by others who've recounted a brush with death, I missed out on an incredible experience. My mind's eye didn't record any information about my near-death experience. In fact, my brain took a four-month hiatus beginning in mid-December 1999. With the record button off, my stroke is lost in a vast abyss with other, more pleasant events including Christmas, my 33rd birthday, and the Y2K non-event.

The paramedics who responded to Troy's 9-1-1 call were apparently flummoxed by my situation. I looked fine, had good vitals, had no signs of drug or alcohol use, and was obviously not an abuse victim. What in the world had happened to me? After talking with Troy, they called an ambulance to transport me to the hospital. Troy automatically specified the hospital where my primary care physician works and where our sons had been born. Fortunately, that hospital is also our local trauma center so the staff's well-prepared to handle the bizarre variety of medical needs they see.

Time is too precious to waste on *what-iffing*, but one what-if does haunt me a bit. *What if* Troy had gone-out with his friends to watch the Super Bowl as so many men do? Our sons might have found me lying lifeless on the bathroom floor. What psychological damage might they have sustained trying to get me to respond, wondering what to do, wishing Dad were home, etc.? That *what-if* makes me eternally thankful Troy was home when my brain imploded.

One bummer about the day's events is that I got to ride in an ambulance but don't remember anything about the trip. The paramedic's records describe me as being unresponsive but capable of breathing on my own. What a miracle my brain remained on speaking terms with my heart and lungs.

When we reached the emergency room, the staff there concurred with the paramedics' opinion—I was unresponsive. Apparently, they saw some other stroke warning signs and ordered a CAT scan. This simple, non-invasive test is often the first step in diagnosing stroke. When a CAT scan of the brain is taken, areas that are darker than normal may not be receiving enough blood, indicating an ischemic stroke. Any white spots may represent areas of the brain covered with blood as the result of a hemorrhage.

My scan was littered with white spots and my medical record says I had an "intraventricular hemorrhage with some subarachnoid hemorrhage." That result was significant because it meant I wasn't a candidate for Tissue Plasminogen Activator (tPA). This clot-busting drug has saved many lives and reduced brain injury among those who survive an ischemic stroke. A key limitation of tPA is that it can only be administered within three hours of the onset of stroke symptoms.

The last thing a hemorrhagic stroke patient needs is **increased** blood flow to the brain. Why invite Niagara Falls to join the frenzy when a random smattering of blood can create adequate destruction?

There was nothing the medical staff could do for me initially, other than admit me, prepare me for a lengthy stay, keep me comfortable, and watch for complications. A feeding tube, PICC line (used when long-term IV will be needed), and catheter were installed. Drugs to reduce the swelling in my brain were added to my IV. The doctor who admitted me gave me a five–ten percent chance of living through the night and made the following note in my medical record:

> "[The patient] arrived at emergency room at 10:37 p.m. and was noted to give no verbal response and had an emergent head CT. She was also noted to have no movement of the left arm and leg. Head CT on review shows filling with blood of all 4 ventricles and some early enlargement of the anterior horns of the temporal lobes..."

This entry summarizes how severe my stroke was. Doctors knew the left-half of my body was paralyzed and suspected I had some underlying cognitive changes. I think the enlargement of the anterior horns noted in this entry means my brain was swelling and beginning to extend through the natural openings in the skull. If that sounds pretty serious to you, you're correct. It was getting a bit too crowded inside my skull and my brain was getting squeezed. That threat may be what prompted my doctors to give me such a slim chance of living.

Perhaps they didn't expect me to see the light of day on Jan. 31 because their opinions were based only on their knowledge of stroke and my test results. Those who know me well and love me, namely Troy and Mom, based their opinions on different information. They know I'm fiercely independent and always up for a good fight. Besides, they'd seen me talk myself through some hefty challenges before. I imagine they knew I could both survive and make a decent recovery with my history in mind.

What they didn't know is that, despite my independence, I've also cried out to God for help when I'm in over my head from as long ago as I can re-

My brain had been loaded with communication skills and experiences for years but nothing really set me apart from others with those skills until my stroke. Suddenly, I had a great story to tell.

member. Somehow, I sensed death wasn't an option for me at that time because I hadn't fulfilled His plan for my life.

When I opened my eyes on Jan. 31, I had no idea where I was or what had happened to me. Most importantly, I didn't know that while flirting with death I'd done something which would turn my pre-stroke life on its ear. I'd chosen to do what Jesus suggests in Matthew 16:24, Mark 8:34, and Luke 9:23. Each of these verses tell us the only way we can be reunited with God at the end of our earthly life is by acknowledging Jesus sacrificed His life on a cross so our sins could be forgiven.

My stroke provided a *time-out* so I could hear what God had to say about getting my life in order. Having a brain hemorrhage is the ultimate *boot to the head*, in my opinion. How sad I ignored God's presence until this medical emergency put my life on hold. Apparently, my stroke cleared my mind and then the Holy Spirit's voice became audible. God didn't cause me to have a stroke but He experienced it with me, and has taken each step of my recovery with me.

My belief that God didn't control whether or not I had a stroke is supported by John 9:1-3, which says, "And as Jesus passed by, he saw a man which was blind from his birth. And his disciples asked him, saying, Master, who did sin, this man, or his parents, that he was born blind? Jesus answered, "Neither hath this man sinned, nor his parents: but that the works of God should be made manifest in him."

Stroke was simply included in God's Master Plan for my life. Some combination of decisions and actions, made by me and an unknown assortment of others, somehow resulted in me having a brain hemorrhage. I don't need to know why or how, I only need to know what God expects me to do next. With that belief, my main question for God is, "What next, Lord?" rather than, "Why me?"

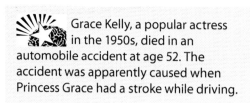
Grace Kelly, a popular actress in the 1950s, died in an automobile accident at age 52. The accident was apparently caused when Princess Grace had a stroke while driving.

CHAPTER 4

DEAD WOMEN
TELL NO TALES

The left half of my body was initially paralyzed but my brain decided to get back on speaking terms with most of that side after about three weeks. Areas of my brain responsible for speech went on strike for three days. Although I now have full use of my left side and can speak clearly, I have numerous cognitive deficits. These invisible losses make my life challenging, tiring, and frustrating. And, that's on a good day.

Mom says that after I knew what was going on (or so she thought), I always wanted someone to put lotion on my face and hands. For variety, I'd ask someone to rearrange my pillows and blankets or adjust the hat I wore to cover my bald head, shorn in preparation for brain surgery. I'm much more into reassuring touches than anyone in my immediate family so this was probably my best shot at getting a hug.

I was used to getting lots of hugs from our young sons and was probably starving for physical contact. These safe interactions may have been the only way I could get the contact

Gee, I wish... ...I'd done my funeral pre-planning.

I craved. Of course God was right there with me but it's not like I could get an actual hug from Him.

I do vaguely recall wondering how in the world anyone gets any rest in a hospital. I had inflatable sock-type things on each leg to minimize the risk of developing a blood clot. These suckers woke me up each time they inflated, going up and down at a pre-set rate. Announcements on the PA system at all hours shocked me, especially the "Pediatric Code Blue" messages because I assumed those meant a child who wasn't breathing would soon arrive at the hospital. Although I was in la-la land, I worried one of our sons might be the youngster in transit.

When my 78-day hospital stint began, neither Troy nor I knew we'd have another *person* (me) to rear when I returned home. In many ways, it was as if we suddenly had a third child. This child had arrived without the traditional 9-month warning, however, and we'd had no introductory classes on handling common challenges.

Troy surely had his hands full, as I was transferred from the emergency room to the Intensive Care Unit (ICU), because I was the one who kept most things running smoothly in our home. My ability to think clearly about multiple, important topics at the same time had sheltered Troy from many crises in the past. Typically, I was the parent who stepped up to address and explain unexpected challenges. I was known for my ability to remain calm and think clearly under extreme pressure. When my brain imploded, everything I'd been doing for myself and our family became Troy's responsibility.

I can't imagine how Troy found the words to tell our sons what had happened to me. My man-of-few-words is painfully honest and really dislikes surprises. There he was, in the hospital, unsure whether I'd live or die, perhaps wondering which option was preferable, knowing our two young sons would soon awaken asking, "Where's Mom?"

My doctors knew I'd sustained a severe injury but there was no way to predict how it would affect me **if** I lived. As a result, I certainly don't hold it against anyone who may have wondered if I would have been better off dead.

Before journeying too far, my brain had to get itself back in order, which would require some miracles. Remember that ten percent chance of living mentioned earlier? Well, my brain's physical condition deteriorated after that outlook was made. It would take the expertise of many skilled medical professionals to rebuild me. Only the Grace of God would make me better than I was before, to (loosely) borrow a line from *The Six Million Dollar Man*.

Mom's journal entry on Feb. 1 shows how closely the doctors watched my brain's reaction to the bleed:

> ### Feb. 1
> They thought E better. Might move out of ICU. Dr. changes his mind. Some more clot they think, Troy and I stayed again in the hospital.

What no one knew was that my stroke had also caused a permanent change in my heart. It's always been physically strong but had a major weakness prior to my stroke. It lacked a connection with God. As I see it, my brain hemorrhage produced enough fertile ground for one of the God seeds I'd acquired in my first 33 years to take root. When my right middle cerebral artery ruptured, I took the first step in my ongoing, spiritual journey.

After recognizing a God seed had sprouted, it took a few more years for me to figure out how to nurture it, due to the severity of my brain injury. God knew I'd take this journey before I was even born and fortunately, He's leading the way.

Biblical parables often strike people differently and the one about a Lamp Under a Basket (Matt 5:14-16; Mark 4:21,22; Luke 8:16,17; and Luke 11:33-36) seems to apply to my situation. This parable tells me that when God equips a person with a gift, He expects the person to use that gift to share the light of His love with others. The gift shouldn't be hidden away or kept out-of-sight. I misused my God-given communication skills for 33 years by spending them to achieve earthly goals.

Suddenly, without warning, those skills were housed within a mute, half-paralyzed body. Not much of an improvement, eh? If you're wondering how I even **survived** the hemorrhage, I'm not aware of any solid medical explanation. I'm thinking it transformed my mind into a prime location for the breath of God I was born with to consume my soul. The energy of this new wind sustained me, prompted me to shift my focus to things above, and helped me keep moving forward. This first step in my spiritual journey happened about six years before I was able to recognize God expects me to invest my time glorifying Him and getting to know Him better.

God also knew that when I could think clearly again, I'd recognize how important it is to make the most of each day by loving, honoring, and cherishing my husband and helping our sons *grow-up great*. After all, the time and talents invested in helping others grow closer to God have eternal, not earthly, value. When it finally *registered*, I knew the answer to the "Why am I here?" question that had haunted me for so long. I'm here to glorify God, grow closer to Him, and encourage others to accept the Salvation provided by Jesus Christ's Death and Resurrection.

> Mom used to can dill pickles each summer. One year, Ron's goldfish died during the canning process, and we attributed Goldie's death to the overwhelming smell of vinegar and dill.

Very few people thought I'd survive my stroke at this time, let alone regain my gift of gab. I can't imagine anyone thought my stroke would transform my life into one focused on matters of eternal, rather than earthly, value. My doctors knew what had happened to my brain but only God knew what had happened in my heart. A heart change like the one I experienced is described in Galatians 2:20, which says, "The life which I now live in the flesh I live by the faith of the Son of God, who loved me, and gave himself for me."

Did it matter I was unaware I was in for the fight of my life? Not in the least. I've had a passionate will to live for as long as I can remember, and what a blessing that's been. My survival instinct had come in handy several times before my stroke. For example, I survived having two quarters extracted from my esophagus, needing rabies shots twice, being chased by a bull, and a host of mindless college antics.

As a mom, I know kids learn how to live by modeling the trusted adults in 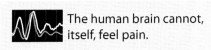 The human brain cannot, itself, feel pain. their life, namely, their parents. Every bit of information that enters a child's mind seems to help mold the type of adult he's becoming. Fighting for my life was my automatic reaction because I instinctively knew Trent and Don were watching me.

Becoming a mom had prompted me to reconsider how important it is to lead by example. Since most children view what the trusted adults in their life do as the right way to do things, I've been aware of the example I set for Trent and Don since each was born. Although we didn't see each other during my three weeks in the ICU, I'm sure Troy and other trusted souls told them I was fighting for my life. These stories surely impacted their view of the world. With our sons watching me, rolling over and playing dead wasn't an option for me. I'm sure I knew (subconsciously) I wanted to show them how to respond when life kicks them in the teeth.

What a blessing that Troy's a man of his word. When he promised to love, honor, and cherish me until we're parted by death, he meant it. I'd always been confident he'd do that for me and Troy was called to put his words into action that night. He suddenly found himself alone in a hospital, not knowing what was wrong with me, providing all of the information needed to have me admitted. I'm sure Troy was also sorting through what he'd tell our sons when he got home.

I'm sure I silently asked God, "Why me? What'd I do to deserve this?" Matthew 27:46 describes how Jesus asked comparable questions, saying, "My God, my God, why hast thou forsaken me?" Clearly God hadn't forsaken Jesus, who died an excruciating death, surrounded by criminals and those mocking Him. He was able to die with dignity asking only that Our Father forgive those who abused and killed Him, because they were ignorant of what they were doing. Nor did Our Father forsake me. He stayed right beside me as I lay battling for my life, unaware anything was even going on.

My three weeks in the ICU would've fascinated me, in a terrifying sort of way. I would've been checking the place out and asking the staff a million questions except for two small problems: my left side was paralyzed and I was mute. As a result, I simply lay on my back, staring blankly ahead of me, except for the time I pulled my feeding tube out with my right hand. Apparently I didn't like having that thing crammed down my throat via my nose. After reinserting the tube, the staff tied my *good* hand to the bed rail to keep me from removing it again.

Isn't it amazing my brain was able to keep me alive even after parts of it had died and other areas were fighting to stay alive? Even better, my memory automatically switched from record to pause when my hemorrhage occurred so that none of the horror I endured would stick with me. Medical professionals I've asked about this blackout period tell me it's a blessing I remember nothing because I was in intense pain. With wiring that good, we humans surely must be made in God's own image (Genesis 1:26).

What Troy didn't know was that my brothers had found a way to get Mom to my bedside as soon as possible. Vic had called Ron after letting our parents know what was happening. They decided that although Ron lives about three hours away, he'd pick Mom up and take her to the hospital. This arrangement allowed for Vic to stay with Troy at the hospital. However, it also required Ron and his wife, Carol, to pack their three young sons into a car at about 5 a.m. for a 3-hour drive to Mom and Dad's.

When Ron's family arrived at our childhood home, Mom was packed and ready to head to the most difficult hospital call she'd ever made. I assume Dad elected to stay home at this time because he wasn't yet prepared to see his baby girl in the condition he'd heard described.

Fortunately, Mom thought to pack a notebook to use as a journal, something she'd always encouraged me to do as a child. Mom is a chronic worrier and seems to fare better when she has something to keep her distracted during troubling times. The thoughts

Mom jotted down in her journal are the only personal information recorded during my hospitalization that I have for reference. Her first post-stroke journal entry says:

Monday, Jan. 31, 2000
Vic called at 12:30 a.m. saying your little girl is in the hospital at Methodist. Vic called back in one hour saying not as bad as they had thought. Vic then called Ron and Ron's picked me up at 7:30 a.m. Ron drove my car and; got to the hospital and E is semi-conscious. Was given many tests (stroke) blood clot on the brain. Troy and I stayed all night at the hospital ICU waiting room.

> **SideNote:** The journal entry above mentions a blood clot on my brain. That clot may have almost killed me or may be what saved my life. If it formed in another part of my body, traveled to my brain, and hit a weak spot in my right middle cerebral artery, it may have caused the hemorrhage. On the flip side, it may have formed in my brain after the hemorrhage to help stop the bleeding, comparable to a scab on the skin's surface. If that was its purpose, it helped minimize the amount of blood spewed over my brain.

Either way, the clot was now causing problems as it crowded my brain inside my skull. Troy is the one who noticed I seemed to be slowing down after I'd been in the ICU for a few days. I'm so grateful he was watching and noticed my decline in time. Do you know someone who'll look-out for you if you're ever unable to look-out for yourself? You may need their advocacy, even if you're under the care of highly skilled medical professionals. Especially if you're unable to speak for yourself.

I couldn't have analyzed my situation back then even if I'd had all my wits about me. It would be months before I learned that a ruptured blood vessel in the brain is an entirely different situation than one under the skin. Our skin is pliable so when a blood vessel ruptures and spills blood under the skin, it simply swells to make more room. Granted, a swollen bruise may hurt for a while but there's usually no permanent damage. In contrast, the brain can't swell much without sustaining irreversible damage. That's because it's protected by the ultimate internal helmet: the skull.

If anyone's accused you of being a bonehead, they're absolutely right. You, like every other human, have an incredible bony structure sitting atop your neck. The skull is your brain's best friend. It's right-sized to hold your grey matter snugly, not tightly, and contains exactly enough cerebral spinal fluid (CSF) to cushion your brain from the skull's rough interior. This design helps keep your brain from sloshing around inside the skull.

However, if there's too much CSF, or other fluid, inside your skull, your brain starts to get squeezed because the skull doesn't expand. This problem is kind of like what happens if you try to freeze water in a glass jar. Both the water and the jar shrink as they get colder but the water shrinks more slowly, thereby creating too much volume for the jar to hold. As a result, the jar eventually breaks. However, if a brain gets too large for the skull protecting it, the brain will rupture before the skull breaks.

When my right middle cerebral artery hemorrhaged, the spilled blood lay trapped inside my skull, causing my brain to swell. This blood had to be removed via an emergency ventriculostomy to prevent my brain from rupturing on Feb. 2, Dad's birthday. As if it weren't rude enough of me to try to die on my brother's birthday, I turned around and repeated the antic for Dad. A terse note in Mom's journal says:

Feb. 2

More tests. Less responsive. We called Ron who came at 1:30 a.m. All the family there. Dad's 67th birthday. Touch and go. Vic came back from Phoenix early, because he had a gut feeling E is worse.

The only solution was to relieve the pressure by reducing the amount of fluid inside my skull. Obviously you don't want to lose any brain cells so it's the excess CSF, and/or blood in my case, that had to go.

Somehow, both Ron and Vic could sense my life was hanging by a thread. Times like this prove the value of strong sibling relationships. Mom's journal entry (below) the day after Dr. Carl, a gifted neurosurgeon, performed my ventriculostomy sums the situation up well.

Incidentally, Mom's call to Ron that morning distracted him from the blueprints he was drafting in case our home needed to be made handicap-accessible. Given the severity of my stroke, he thought it best to make plans early on for modifying our home with ramps and rails. Thankfully, his plans weren't needed.

On a purely cosmetic note, I'd like to mention I still had long hair in January of 2000. You may recall Dad wanted me to keep my hair long as a child and I'd never bothered to **really** get it cut after leaving for college. By the time I was 33, my wavy, dark-blonde locks were almost waist-length.

I made up for lost time when my head was unceremoniously shaved in preparation for the ventriculostomy. Before I tell you what a ventriculostomy is, hear me: **Do not try this at home.** A neurosurgeon may perform an emergency ventriculostomy if a patient's brain is in imminent danger of rupturing, which is as bad as it sounds. A ventriculostomy involves having a hole drilled through the skull and a drainage tube threaded from the affected ventricle(s) to the outside world. This tube allows excess CSF, or blood in my case, to drain out.

Things started looking up a bit the next day when I blurted out my first word post-stroke. When I learned to talk as a baby, my first word was *ma-ma*, but I went with *water*, this time around. It's nice to know my favorite drink made a strong impression on my brain pre-stroke. Incidentally, this was the second time in my life I began talking before walking. Loved ones say it took a couple of weeks for me to begin speaking clearly

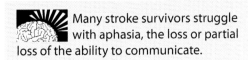

Many stroke survivors struggle with aphasia, the loss or partial loss of the ability to communicate.

again. Mom's journal entry on Feb. 4 says:

Feb. 4
Seemed better. Talked some to a nurse.
Ron's went home in p.m.

Clear speech is a challenge for any stroke survivor who suffers from aphasia, a deficit which makes it difficult or impossible for the person to speak clearly and/or to understand spoken words. Although I don't have aphasia, my cognitive losses do affect my ability to communicate clearly and concisely. A speech pathologist who helped me relearn to speak explained that *higher-level cognitive skills* are needed for a person to **succinctly** make her point.

There are many types of higher-level cognitive skills, each of which requires various parts of the brain to work together well. Some of the areas in my brain responsible for language must still be out-of-order because I continue to battle what I call *I'm Talking and I Can't Shut-Up Syndrome*. Writing this book has helped me become more concise, perhaps because I really dislike typing. Babbling senselessly is one thing but there's no way I want to type every word that crosses my mind. Fortunately, I have the rest of my life to get better and I expect I'll become more concise over time.

The medical folks obviously gave my brain all the attention it needed while I was in the ICU, however, they neglected to take seriously a problem brewing in my right arm. The spot where the PICC line was inserted into that arm had become infected, and by Feb. 7 had been festering for several days. My primary care physician, Dr. Hiram, discovered this problem during a courtesy visit at about 6 a.m. that day. He had apparently stopped to see me at least daily to help comfort my family and ensure I was getting the best possible care. Dr. Hiram had gently squeezed my right arm at the end of each office visit I'd had since he began treating my underactive thyroid at age 12.

When he squeezed my arm at the end of this visit, he noticed it was unusually warm and asked the nurse what was going on. She assured Dr. Hiram the staff knew about the infection and was watching it but he insisted my arm needed immediate attention. Mom's journal entry about this concern says:

Feb. 7
No change. Squeezed with right hand. About this time got infection in arm from IV. Dr. Hiram alarmed the nurses.

When this problem finally got the attention it deserved, I was within minutes of blood poisoning, which generally leads to immediate death. A vascular surgeon, Dr. Tom, did emergency surgery that day to remove two dead blood vessels in my arm. He removed about 18 inches from just below my elbow extending up into my arm pit, and back down. The scars on my arm confirm what I've heard about Dr. Tom making incisions every two inches along the way. Apparently, the vessels were so deteriorated they snapped each time he tried to extract them. Each time the vessel broke, Dr. Tom had to go back in again a couple of inches farther along the route.

My arm was so infected, it's a wonder Dr. Tom was able to save my life, let alone my arm. I'm told the stench was so intense when he made the first incision, he had to leave the operating room momentarily because he thought he was going to vomit. Not good. This surgery also required me to get three units of blood. I've been a dedicated blood donor since age 18, so there's a chance some of the blood I received came from my most recent donation. What goes around does come around, doesn't it?

As he worked, Dr. Tom inserted metal pegs at each end of the incisions and connected them with a rubber band-type strand, under my skin. When I retuned to my ICU room, my right arm was held upright in a sling so the infection would drain more effectively. Nurses visited my room regularly to jiggle these pegs so the infection would stay loose and drain more freely. Mom's journal says:

Feb. 8
Arm is doing well. Is in a sling held upright.

This whole concept is, in a word, gross. Can you even imagine what my arm looked like that day? The *cruel* irony here is that my **left** arm was paralyzed. If the infection had been on that side, I wouldn't have needed any anesthetic and might have been able to entertain myself picking scabs. But no... it was my **right** arm, so hello anesthetic and goodbye entertainment. Ah well. At least it wasn't a loved one's birthday this time.

The staff used scar massage, a special drainage technique, and some funky bandages to keep the infection from returning and to keep my scars pliable. A couple of years later, I remembered hearing about a product used to lighten skin and tracked down a bottle.

My arm looks much better now and, as I tell our sons, "Hey, I still have my arm and I have the best identifiable marks of any mom in the county." The only real difference I notice is that my right arm now gets cold very easily. When wearing short sleeves, I often keep my right arm bundled in an arm warmer, a *stylish* accessory that resembles those worn by some football players.

When combined with some memories of my hospitalization provided by my dear friend (Helen), Mom's journal entries become profound. Helen's assistant interrupted her during an important meeting on Jan. 31 to tell her I'd been taken to the hospital the previous evening after suffering a massive stroke. Ironically, Helen and I knew a young man who was still hospitalized from the stroke he'd suffered, when I had mine. In her words, "It seemed like just too much!"

Helen recalls visiting me in the hospital that day and most of the following days, and feeling very frightened for me. She's one of those souls who's always composed but she told me a few years post-stroke that, "Sadness and fear are a powerful combination." I think that was her way of telling me my situation had reduced (even) her to tears.

Troy had regular conversations with Helen, who describes him as being lost but composed. Many of their conversations included stories about how much I mean to them. She also talked with Mom, who although the polar opposite of Helen, was experiencing similar emotions. Helen describes Mom as being so scared that at times she barely made sense. Been there… seen that… not a good thing. These three key souls were deeply worried about whether or not I'd live. An even deeper worry was at what level I'd be able to function if I did survive.

Helen said, in retrospect, "When I was not with you, sometimes I cried. You were so young and so bright and so vibrant. I couldn't bear to see you so helpless and not there. I was afraid you'd die. And, I was afraid you wouldn't be the same if you lived."

Troy had another *crisis* to handle in mid-February. Mookie, the white cat mentioned earlier, had been crying a lot. Mookie had feline leukemia, a terminal cat disease, but had lived well with it for more than 12 years. Unfortunately, it took hold and began shutting her body down early in 2000. By mid-February it had caused her liver to stop functioning and she was in great pain. Troy knew that if I'd been home, I'd have had her euthanized when the time came, so that's what he did. He also knew I'd have asked my dad to bury her near the kitties I'd grown-up with, so Troy called my dad and asked if he'd be willing to bury the Mookster.

Dad told Troy he was welcome to drop her off. When Troy took my beloved *nurse cat* to our vet to have her euthanized, Dr. Ron's first question was, "Where's E?" He knows I'm the one who generally handles upsetting situations such as that. While answering Dr. Ron, Troy mentioned he knew euthanizing Mookie was what I would have done if I could. He then drove an hour to my parents' home to drop-off Mookie's body. Dad had already dug her grave, next to her long-time buddy, George.

Troy then returned to the hospital to tell me of her death, and says I cried when he broke the news. When I grasped the significance of this story a few years post-stroke, I was overcome with emotion… and gratitude. Having Mookie *planted* next to Georgie was exactly what I'd have chosen, if I'd been in a position to handle her final days. How many men would have done something so considerate for their wife while she lay (potentially) dying in a hospital?

My fight for life started to pay off about now as Mom's journal entries show:

Feb. 9
More responsive, but not talking. Started moving left leg.

Feb. 10
Serious now. 50/50 chance. Fed some applesauce and pudding.

Feb. 12
Smiled and yawned. Not much change. Started moving left leg and left arm.

Feb. 13
Talked to Mom and ate soft food well today. Had 2 units of blood. Not much change.

Feb. 14
Said 9 words. Ate good was wakeful.

Feb. 15
Not as responsive. Dad was up. Wasn't draining fast enough.

Feb. 16
Changed brain tube in head. More responsive.

Feb. 17
Shut-off drainage tube from the brain. Started solid food and ate good, responsive.

Feb. 18
Took drainage tube out from head. Could be out of ICU but

no bed on Floor 5. Was responsive and talked twice to Troy.

Barry, one of my ICU nurses, made quite an impression on Troy. As I recall, Troy credits Barry with giving him reason to hope for my survival and recovery. My doctors didn't think I'd live, let alone recover, but something told Barry I had a shot. Perhaps that's because he got to know my loved ones and me so well. Whatever the reason, I deeply appreciate the support he provided for Troy.

I visited the doctor's office where Barry now works to personally thank him, eight years post-stroke. Although he'd cared for hundreds, perhaps thousands, of patients during his years as an ICU nurse, Barry remembered me immediately and promptly asked how Troy was doing.

During my three weeks in intensive care, I began overcoming my paralysis and speaking difficulties. Although an occasional break in the day-to-day routines of life can be rejuvenating, time spent recovering from a major medical event is more like a rebirthing. I use that comparison very deliberately because, speaking from experience, childbirth is painful. Rebirthing oneself is excruciating.

When my condition stabilized, after about three weeks, it was time to move me to the rehab area. The left half of my body was still paralyzed, but was showing signs of *waking up* and I was regaining the ability to do some *activities of daily living* (ADL), such as feeding myself. An entry in my medical record also lists the ability to help transfer myself from bed to wheelchair and back as an ADL. Fortunately, a wheelchair was needed in my daily routine for only a brief period of time. The medical record entry made when I left the ICU says:

"Although she had improved, her left hemiparesis remained and she was transferred to the rehabilitation center on 2/25/00 in a stable condition."

It's still hard to fathom how my loved ones knew I was near death and I didn't have a clue. They may have also wondered if perhaps death might be the best solution to my predicament. If so,

I certainly understand and don't hold that against them. After all, there was no way to predict how my brain injury would affect me if I did live. My doctors knew only that it was a severe injury and several areas of my brain had likely been affected.

Joseph Kennedy, Sr., an American political figure, died of stroke at 81.

CHAPTER 5

DOIN' TIME ON
CLOUD EIGHT

Once again, some of my mom's comments, from her daily *Watch over E* diary, to get things started.

Saturday, Feb. 19
Moved to neurology area. Sat up for first time (20 minutes). Heart started beating fast. Was in ICU 20 or 21 days.

Feb. 22
Much better, talked to Dad on phone, many sentences.

Feb. 23
Still improving, Trent (elder son) visited for first time.

Feb. 24
Good in AM but mixed up in PM. Don (younger son) visited the first time.

Gee, I wish... ...I'd convinced Troy to build a home in the country.

Feb. 25
Moved to rehab area.

Saturday, Feb. 26
Dad visits. She was not very responsive. Ron visits.

Feb. 27
Very alert until 1:30 p.m. Slept 3 hours and mixed up; Dad visits.

Feb. 28
Alert all a.m. PT twice, speech and OT.

Feb. 29
Speech not as good. Walked some.

March 1
Speech and memory loss. Fed herself and walked some with help, much improved in PT.

My three weeks in the ICU provided time and space for my brain to start getting itself back together. Moving to the rehab area of the hospital was the first, big step in my ongoing recovery. My therapy experiences there are described in the next chapter. This chapter describes how I got to the bottom of the most confounding mystery of my life.

Dr. Denny must have thought I had a pretty good grasp of what had happened to me and what was going on. I had him fooled; he was eating from the palm of my hand. I had no idea where I was, how I'd gotten there, or what was next for me. I'd been in a sort of la-la land for several weeks, hence the reference to Cloud 8 in this chapter title. Let's just say the time recuperating from a stroke isn't exactly time on Cloud 9.

Translated, the medical record entry about my move day means I'd started speaking again and the left side of my body was showing some signs of life. One *minor* hurdle impeding my transfer was that I'd been lying down for about three weeks. Dr. Denny had me transferred to the neurology area for a few days to see how I'd respond to my first therapy *activity*, which seems almost laughable now. The nurses there jacked my bed up to see how my body would respond to a change in altitude after lying flat on my back for so long.

Troy says my blood pressure shot up when I first went vertical. That's not all bad given my BP has averaged 90/60 since I was a teen. Apparently the nurses helped me repeat that *strenuous* activity for a few days until they felt I was ready for my move to the rehab area.

It was around this time my brain decided to start acting more like it had before my stroke. Although I'm curious by nature, I seemed to lose interest in what was going on around me when my brain imploded. Go figure. As a result, I'd been hospitalized for three weeks and had no idea anything out-of-the-ordinary had happened.

As my brain adjusted to the reorganization which had occurred at its cellular level, my curiosity began to return, and I started to notice some oddities around me. First off, it seemed unusual most of the people I saw were dressed in white and many others were bald. Clues #1 and #2 in the great puzzle.

Clue #3 was that these white-clad people kept asking me inane questions, such as:

- What's your name? **Got this one right.**
- Do you know why you're here and what happened to you? **Must have dodged this one.**
- How many children do you have? **Told folks we have three sons. Since we have two, this was wishful thinking.**
- How old are you? **Assume I said 22, since that's the age which still comes to mind first. Twenty-two must have been a great age for me, because I was 33 at the time.**
- When's your birthday? **Got that one right. Ding-ding-**

ding-ding!

- What building are we in? **Probably dodged this one, too.**
- What city and state are we in? **Assume I guessed these correctly.**
- What day is it? **Probably dodged this question.**
- What do you remember about February? **Told a therapist it comes after January and before March. Apparently this wasn't the answer she was looking for but it was the best I could do. I had to rely on my long-term memory of what February is because I had no idea what I'd been doing in February of 2000.**
- Who's the president? **The therapist must have been a Democrat because my answer of *Brother Bill* didn't get a chuckle. Never one to give up easily, though, I changed my answer to Ross Perot. She looked so concerned I finally added, "Well, he almost made it didn't he?"**

In addition to their unflattering attire and limited conversation skills, these poor souls had to enforce a toileting schedule to re-expand my bladder. Clue #4 amounted to the therapists telling me I could use the toilet only once every three hours. Apparently, the catheter I'd had while in the ICU had caused my bladder to shrink during its *time off*.

A toileting schedule is a necessary evil for anyone who's been catheterized for a length of time because when the catheter is removed, the bladder has to start doing its own work again. This means it has to stretch to accommodate the amount of liquid it needs to store.

This 3-hour schedule obviously made an impression on me because I recall desperately telling whomever would listen that I was about to wet my wheelchair. Somehow I knew that would create work for the staff so surely they'd help me to the bathroom. Right?

Wrong! They knew I didn't want to wet myself and, by golly,

they were right. So I'd sit there in terror, hoping desperately that my three hours were almost up. Then one day, it occurred to me no nurse in his right mind would want to clean a **soiled** wheelchair. From that day forward, I'd hold it as long as I could and then urgently tell the staff I needed to go #2. That got 'em moving! The benefits for me were obvious. When #2 goes, #1 will follow.

> **Score**
> E — 1
> Nursing staff — 0

Okay, so I cheated. At least I was thinking *strategically* again. I did almost get busted one day when a nurse asked if I'd had a good BM. After asking her what a BM is, I pointed out that bowel movements stink, whether they're *good* or not. Unfortunately, my snide remark prompted her to notice the biffy didn't stink. Me and my big mouth...

These clues were floating around in my mind when I awoke one morning to find myself gazing into the eyes of a man I didn't recognize. As I scanned my brain for information about why a man other than my husband would be looking at me in bed, he said, "Do you always sleep on your back?" I automatically said, "No, I always sleep on my side." (This is not a convincing answer when you're lying flat on your back looking up at someone.)

The man said, "You can still sleep on your side, you know. You can even sleep on your right side. It isn't going to hurt anything." Why would anyone tell me it was okay to sleep on my right side? That's not something any sane adult would say, is it? Little did I know, this conversation was with Dr. Denny, my physiatrist (AKA physical rehab doctor). As he walked away I started thinking how odd his comments had been. The whole interaction had been so weird I decided it was time for me to figure out what was going on.

I knew what I wanted to ask but was unsure whom I should ask. After all, if you're questioning your own sanity, what benefit is there in drawing attention to your concern?

Fortunately, Troy has always been truthful with me so I resolved to ask him my question the next time he visited. When he stopped by on his way to work that morning, I said, "I have a question for you." Then I paused, prompting Troy to say, "You can ask me anything; you know I'll tell you the truth." So tell me something I don't know! Like the answer to the question I was mulling over. Somehow, it seemed like such an odd question, I told him I'd ask him later.

We repeated this scenario during each of his morning and afternoon visits for several days. Finally, one afternoon, Troy said, "Just ask me, will you? This question thing is driving me crazy!" When I told him I didn't want anybody to come in and overhear us talking, he said, "Well you're gonna have to ask me here 'cause it's not like I can check you out." Check me out? Wasn't quite sure what he meant by that... Was I being held captive or something?

To ease his anxiety, I told Troy I'd call him that night after the boys were in bed. Obviously my brain was starting to process information again because I knew it'd be better for Troy if our sons were asleep when he took my phone call. Somehow, I sensed my question might rock his world.

Along about 9 p.m., I grabbed the phone from the table by my bed and dialed our home phone number. When Troy answered the phone, my first question was, "Are the boys in bed?" He confirmed Trent and Don were in bed so I asked, "Are you sitting down?" Troy said, "No, do I need to be?" I was sitting down so I figured he should be, too. Only after Troy said, "Okay. I'm sitting down. Now what is your question?!?" did I ask, in the calmest voice I could muster, "Why am I here?" Let me tell you, that's an effective way to stall a conversation. I wasn't asking in the philosophical sense. I just wanted to know why the heck I was in whatever physical location I happened to be in. I resisted the urge to ask for clarification on exactly where I was...

My husband, always a man of few words, was stone silent for what seemed an eternity before saying nonchalantly, "Are you asking me why you're in the hospital or why you're in rehab?" I'm thinkin', huh? Why would I be in the hospital? I'm not pregnant, far as I know. And why would I need rehab? I've never even experimented with illegal drugs and (used to) drink maybe a beer a week. His response didn't exactly answer my question but it did help keep our conversation moving along.

Finally, I said, "You can answer either question. I'm sure I'll have more." The words he said next changed my life forever. My beloved husband of (almost) nine years said, "You remember you had a stroke, right?" Okay, that tops my attempt at asking the mother of all stalling questions. As I sat there in my hospital bed, shocked out of my wits, I felt this incredible calmness overtake me.

That was the first time in my life I felt God's presence right beside me. After a long pause, I pushed back, "What'd ya mean I had a stroke?" Troy knows me well enough that his immediate response was, "E, before I say another word, you've got to believe me. We've all been telling you the truth, the whole truth, and nothing but the truth from the very beginning, and we thought you knew." My only response was, "I had a what?"

After repeating, "You had a stroke," Troy explained what had happened to me over the past 10+ weeks. I just sat there. Stricken… thinking… wondering what to do next. The question I'd been dying to ask had backfired, to say the least. I had assumed Troy would tell me the truth, and had no back-up plan in mind for getting 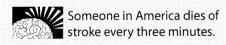 Someone in America dies of stroke every three minutes. the information I so desperately wanted. I wondered what other women do if their husband *lies* to them.

Duh! They ask their mom. So… after ending my call to Troy, I called Mom. I remembered my folks' unlisted number, but a sappy computer voice told me I couldn't make a long distance call from the phone I was using. Thankfully, I remembered hearing about a long distance service that might help.

I'd never used it before but dialed the number (stored in my long-term memory) with great anticipation. A kindly computer voice said I could either place a collect call or charge my call to a credit card or calling card. Somehow I figured Mom wouldn't appreciate me making a collect call so I picked the latter option.

The nice e-voice then said to dial my home phone number. No

problem. After that, it said to enter my credit card number. Oh crap! I didn't have my purse with me. Worse yet, I didn't even have a store receipt with my card number on it.

Okay, so I needed another option. Apparently, I'd done a bit too much Internet shopping prior to my stroke because I was fairly confident I knew my 16-digit credit card number. I entered that number and BINGO—I was in! Until the e-voice said to enter my card's 4-digit expiration date. Got that right, too.

Then came the test of all tests. The e-voice said to enter that stupid, 3-digit security code from the back of my card. You know the one. The number you never remember when you really need to charge something and your card isn't handy? Okay, so I got that right, too. The advantages of online shopping go on and on and on...

Although I overlooked the significance of this feat at the time, I think this was the first proof my long-term memory is intact.

> Remember when the credit card number you used to make a purchase was printed on most store receipts? Those days seem long ago now. But then...Social Security Numbers used to be printed on drivers licenses, too. Golly the world's changed a lot since 1966.

It probably scared Mom's bi-jibblins out of her to get a phone call that late in the evening with me in the hospital but I was on a quest for vital information. Our conversation started with me stating in a frightened, whiney voice, "Mom, you're not gonna believe what Troy just told me." After listening to a summary of my previous phone call, Mom confirmed what Troy had told me and added some information of her own. Strike 2. So what's a woman supposed to do when her husband and her mom are in cahoots? Call a friend.

My mind was racing as I dialed my friend, Kari's, number. She and I had worked together for years and I was sure I could trust her. Fortunately, I caught Kari at home that evening. She listened patiently as I told her what Troy and Mom had told me before confirming everything they'd said and adding her own bits of information. Strike 3. Life gets pretty tough when your husband, your mom, and a close friend are working together to drive you crazy. However, I'm an eternal optimist and felt I had one last shot at getting to the bottom of my dilemma.

Someone nice seemed to always appear in my room soon after I pushed a certain button on the rail of the bed, and I pushed it frantically. A white-clad woman appeared in my doorway almost immediately asking, "Did you need something, E?" I replied, "I 'spose you think I had a stroke, too?" This nurse obviously knew me well because she had the ultimate response. She chuckled. That's right… she chuckled at my question. Then she said, "Yeah, well you know, you have been here a while."

All I could say was, "No, I don't know." She then proceeded to tell me what Troy, Mom, and Kari had just shared with me. Game over? Not yet. I wasn't about to let her off the hook that easily. Instead, I said, "Okay, so maybe I had a stroke but the last time I checked strokes had nothing to do with arms. How in the world did I get all these scars on my arm?" This patient woman even had an answer for how my right arm had become so *distinctive*. She then said she needed to get back to the nurses' station and calmly walked away.

I coined the term *BrainBuzz* to describe the overwhelming cognitive feeling I've had each time a cognitive connection restores itself. It takes a day or two for me to think clearly again after getting one of these intense sensations.

Words cannot describe how I felt as the reality of my situation began to settle-in. As I thought about things, I realized I had no better explanation for my situation and, worse yet, couldn't remember anything that had happened over the past several weeks. To say I had a tough time falling to sleep that night would be a gross understatement. Fortunately, God's presence at my side was almost tangible, and I eventually fell asleep with Him watching over me.

Needless to say, Troy and I didn't make much small talk when he stopped by the next morning.

Helen says when she stopped by later that day, I said, "You'll never guess what I found out last night. I had a stroke! When I asked Troy why I was here, he said I'd had a stroke." Helen assured me she knew I'd had a stroke and had, in fact, visited me at least once each day since Jan. 30. She says I seemed rather shocked by the information I'd gathered the night before. Better believe I was shocked. Back then, I was one of those people who could tell you, without much thought, what I'd been doing every hour of every day for the past several days.

> **SideNote:** It was several months later when Troy told me he'd been worried the question I'd waited so long to ask him might be, "Who are you?" He said he'd felt some relief the morning before I popped the big question when he realized I must know who he is if I knew his telephone number and realized I should call only after our sons were in bed.

Gradually I was coming to terms with the fact I couldn't personally account for several weeks of time and that what I'd heard from others wasn't too appealing. Helen also recalls noticing that day that I seemed to have no realization of the time so many people had spent with me in my time of need. One incredible, and tragic, irony of brain injury is that the medical professionals who save the life of a person with a brain injury, and the loved ones who spend time at his bedside, are often lost in a great abyss because the patient retains no memories for a period of time after the injury.

These conversations occurred on day 75 of my 78-day hospital stay.

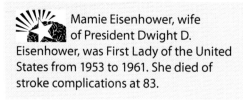

Mamie Eisenhower, wife of President Dwight D. Eisenhower, was First Lady of the United States from 1953 to 1961. She died of stroke complications at 83.

CHAPTER 6

RECOVERY IS
A BUMPY ROAD

God tells us in Ecclesiastes 3 there's a season for everything, "…and a time to every purpose under the heaven." This book of Scripture has a different tone than much of the Bible. Perhaps the author was near the end of life and wishing for more time on Earth? Regardless, I see Ecclesiastes as God's way of telling us to keep our life's events in perspective. When you acknowledge you aren't in control of the universe, or even your tiny corner of it, you can approach each day with a healthy que sera sera (whatever will be, will be) attitude. After all, sin has controlled this world since Eve took that first bite of forbidden fruit in the Garden of Eden. Ultimately, God will determine what becomes of this world, but He's letting us exercise our free will, rather than micro-managing us. He also knows when the events that will end this world, as spelled-out in the book of Revelation, will occur.

In addition to saying there's a time to be born and die, Ecclesiastes 3 mentions several emotions each of us will likely experience in this life. These emotions will be linked with

Gee, I wish… …I'd visited a brain injury rehab center.

events which unfold according to God's plan for our life. These events will likely include a time for us to weep and laugh; mourn and dance; get and lose; and love and hate. The most important thing to remember is that God has a plan for your life and everything, the good and the not-so-good, fits somewhere in His plan.

God's plan called for me to spend from Feb. 25 through April 18, 2000, regaining some control over the connections between my brain and body. To accomplish this, I was transferred to the rehab area of the hospital for in-patient therapy. The therapy sessions I participated in during my eight weeks there provided the structure needed to get my brain back on speaking terms with my body.

My therapy sessions lasted from sunrise to sunset every day during my 8-week stay in the hospital's rehab area. Mom's journal entries from this time include:

E told speech therapists:

She lives in *Timbuktu*—This is my hometown, not where I lived at the time.

She has 3 boys—I'd always hoped to have three sons…

The wrong dates for boys' birthdays—No idea what I said, or why I got these wrong.

Was staying in the hospital where she was born—At least I named a hospital.

Dad is her husband—There's no hidden meaning behind the fact I said my dad's name instead of Troy's.

Many other wrong answers

My in-patient therapy focused on helping me relearn basic skills. It didn't make me the woman I'd been pre-stroke, though. That woman was dead-and-gone.

Mom stayed 50 days straight. Troy came twice a day. Many

from hometown came to ICU to be with my family.

Many of your college friends and colleagues, as well as Troy's, visited. Several people came to be with Troy during your surgeries.

I have scant memories of this *season* in my life, which is probably a blessing. What good would it do to recall how frightening it must be to learn to walk? Especially when you're almost six feet tall? The challenges and humiliation of adult *potty training*? The anxiety of being left alone seated in a wheelchair? Wondering why anyone would be so insulting as to post a sign on my door identifying my room, and a detailed list of what I was going to do every moment of every day?

> **SideNote:** About this time, I recall hearing some nurses talking about when I'd be DC'd. The only thing I could think this meant was deceased, and it seemed rather rude and inconsiderate of them to discuss my death in front of me. Turns out *DC'd* is short-hand for discharged.

Often, some of a stroke survivor's abilities return as her brain adjusts to the injury it sustained. These *spontaneous recoveries* can often be enhanced by speech, physical, occupational, recreational, and other types of therapy. When I started rehab, my therapists' first task was to figure out what was *wrong* with me. My impairments were a bit convoluted because I had a hemorrhagic, rather than ischemic, stroke. This type of brain injury is a bit nebulous because multiple areas of the brain are often affected.

Although I don't have a list of the injured areas in my brain, I can tell you my stroke cleared my mind, quite literally. The **upside** of purging my mind is described later. On the downside, some key abilities suddenly become extinct. Even worse, my brain injury made it difficult for me to recognize what had changed. I've learned it's fairly common for those close to someone who has a brain injury to notice changes in the survivor before she notices them herself. That's one Catch22 of brain injury; having a brain injury makes it difficult or impossible for a person to recognize her brain has been injured.

> Figuring out how my brain injury impacts my life reminds me of a time my mom lost her glasses. She couldn't see well enough to **really** look for them but she did her best. After getting frustrated, she asked me to help. I looked at her in amazement because her glasses were perched atop her head. She put them there so she couldn't possibly lose them! In my situation, it's tough to figure out the impact of my injury because my brain doesn't process information *normally*.

It was painfully obvious to my therapists that stroke had robbed me of some abilities most folks take for granted. Specifically, I couldn't speak clearly and had very limited use of my left side. By the Grace of God, these abilities had returned spontaneously. It's important to note that although dead brain cells aren't replaced, surviving cells may assume some of the responsibilities of their deceased buddies.

The brain may also resume some activities it did automatically pre-injury as the survivor adjusts to her life with a brain injury. As I see it, this recovery is possible because when a brain is injured, activities which aren't necessary for keeping the person alive *shift into neutral*. As the injured brain adjusts to itself, some of the surviving cells may shift back into *drive*.

My first spontaneous recovery feat was saying the word *water* three days post-stroke. I gradually regained my speaking ability by making more complete comments and, eventually, by asking questions. This experience helped me realize that asking a question, even a simple one, requires lots of cognitive energy. Asking a meaningful question requires background knowledge of the topic and an understanding of what information is needed. After identifying that information, you have to figure out who can provide that information. Next you arrange the right time, place, and type of interaction to ask the question. Lastly, you figure out how to ask the question so you'll likely get the answer you seek.

Good grief! Is it any wonder my ability to ask a question began returning after I mastered making simple statements? It tires me, even now, to think of the cognitive energy involved in asking Troy the "Why am I here?" question described earlier. Now I understand why young children so often simply ask, "Why?"

My second spontaneous recovery feat had occurred about three weeks later when I began moving my left arm and leg. I'm so thankful for that miracle. Having the left side of my body paralyzed isn't a challenge I'd want to awaken to for the rest of my life. My therapists, encouraged by these early signs of life, focused on improving communication between the injured areas of my brain and the left side of my body soon after I moved to the rehab area. Technically, my physical therapy (PT) had started soon after my admission to the hospital, but I'd played no role in it.

It's generally in a stroke survivor's best interest to start rehabilitation therapy as soon as possible.

With my left half paralyzed, physical therapists had visited my ICU room regularly to manually rotate my left arm. This *exercise* helped prevent my arm from becoming locked in the shoulder socket. Rotating the joints of a patient lying prone in her bed, **just in case** she lives, and **just in case** the paralysis on that side of her body abates, strikes me as a rather thankless job. Fortunately, my move to the rehab area opened up a whole new world of exercise options for my physical therapists, Tammy C. and Tammy G. For starters, they taught me to transfer to and from a wheelchair with minimal assistance.

This is no small challenge when a patient has been lying down for three weeks and isn't exactly petite. Team Tammy doubtless gained some critical insight of the task-at-hand the first time they flopped my legs over the side of the bed and had to catch me as I fell over the side. That's when we realized my stroke had severely impacted my balance. It'd be nice if that problem were fully resolved by now but um… no.

From then on, Team Tammy secured a gait belt around my waist at the beginning of each PT session. That's *gait*, as in **walking gait**, you know. This heavy-duty leather strap is worn somewhat loosely so a physical therapist can keep a hand under it as the patient moves. The belt makes it easier for the therapist to help the patient regain balance if things get off-kilter during therapy. A gait belt isn't a fashion accessory, that's for sure. A therapist can also use the gait belt to cue the patient to move a certain way, which is helpful if a patient has trouble following verbal cues, as I did.

With my gait belt securely fastened, it took only one Tammy to help me transfer safely to/from the wheelchair. This was a big step toward reclaiming some independence for the nursing staff and me. Until I mastered this feat, at least two medical folks had to be at my side whenever I needed to transfer.

One specific memory I have of Team Tammy is that they never let well enough alone. Whenever I met one of the PT goals they set for me, they immediately raised the bar by challenging me to accomplish something else. They must buy into the saying: If your goal is to be average and you succeed, what have you done? If your goal is to be perfect and you fail, what have you done?

For example, transferring from the bed to the wheelchair quickly translated into moving from the wheelchair to the biffy. Did you know it's a bit scary to hoist yourself from a wheelchair to a small, white oval poised mysteriously above a pool of water? This task was complicated by the fact I had no depth perception at the time. I couldn't tell if I was aiming for a small seat with a hole above the Atlantic Ocean or a small seat above a puddle. Either way, I was taking the proverbial shot in the dark on those transfers.

Then there was the time Team Tammy decided I needed to relearn to climb stairs. The PT room had a set of fake stairs—a simple wooden structure with five steps, the obligatory railings, and a small platform at the top. As I recall, it took Team Tammy almost a week to convince me I really could climb those stairs without tumbling to my death. During that week, I heard them say, "Up with the bad and down with the good," a million or so times. This guidance is important because when coming down the stairs, gravity causes you to pick-up speed and it's important to have your good leg ready to bring things to a halt. They'd throw in the occasional, "Look left," now and then just to keep things interesting.

This reminder helped me accommodate for *left neglect*, a deficit resulting from injury to the right side of the brain, which causes me to overlook the half of the world located to my left. Conversely, an injury in the left hemisphere can cause *right neglect*. An injury in the right hemisphere usually causes more severe neglect, however. My neglect deficit affects all five of my senses but is most noticeable with my vision.

After making Team Tammy swear they wouldn't let me die, and making sure my gait belt was secured, I carefully traversed the steps and reached the *landing*. You'd have thought I'd scaled Mt. Everest. Time to celebrate? Oh no... Team Tammy had other plans. They looked at me calmly and one said, "Now turn around and come back down."

After safely reaching my point of origin, a Tammy asked, "How many steps do you have in your home?" That was an easy question because I'd counted our stairs every time I'd walked them with a baby in my arms. I said, "Well, coming down we have 7, 7, and 5. Going up we have 5, 7, and 7." Apparently they were used to two-story houses because my answer befuddled them. They felt better after I explained our floor plan.

One other memorable PT event occurred when Team Tammy told me to show them I could get down on my hands and knees and then stand back up without assistance. Apparently, brain injury patients must demonstrate this ability before visiting home for the first time. That made sense to me when I recalled a TV commercial from my childhood with an elderly lady shrieking, "Help! I've fallen, and I can't get up!"

Hey, if getting down on the floor and back up was the only thing between me and a visit home, I was ready to *take the plunge.* Unfortunately, that's exactly what I did. Remember that little balance problem described earlier? Turned out I also have a problem with being impulsive, a rather common challenge for those living with a right hemisphere injury. Neither Tammy even had a chance to grab my gait belt as I fell to my left, twisted my knee, and landed in a heap. Ouch!

Then I realized... my left knee hurt. I'd twisted it and it hurt, by gum. You know life's a bit off-kilter when pain is a good thing, but speaking from personal experience, pain beats paralysis any day.

My morning PT session lasted from 8:30—9:30, Monday through Friday. Nothing like getting the tough work out of the way right after breakfast. **If** I survived the morning session, I *got* to return for another hour of PT at 2. When Team Tammy was done *terrorizing* me each morning, I'd wheel off for 30 minutes of recreational therapy with Jenna. Let me assure you, this form of therapy is far more than fun and games. Rec therapy employs *fun* activities to help those with a physical, mental, and/or emotional disability develop the skills needed for daily living and social interactions. Eventually, these new skills may lead to increased independence.

It was Jenna who helped me start figuring out my stroke had left me with the social graces of a goat. A bit blunt perhaps, but you get the picture. To give you an idea of how rec therapy works, imagine ten young adults with brain injuries standing in a circle and the therapist tells them to bump a beach ball around the circle as quickly as possible. The rules were that everyone must bump the ball once only and if it left our circle we had to start over. My group immediately begins blasting the ball around the circle at about warp seven. Unfortunately, this approach resulted in us breaking both rules almost immediately.

In some situations, this activity might present the opportunity for one person to show favoritism toward another. You know what I mean. Everyone wants to bump the ball to the good-looking man or woman. With this group, only deep concentration was visible on each person's face as we tried to remember who'd already bumped the ball. No time for fooling around here; this was serious business.

After several failed attempts, someone pointed out it might be easier for us to meet Jenna's expectations if each of us simply bumped the ball to the person on our right instead of relying on our (lame) short-term memories and bumping it around at random. This suggestion came as a bit of a shock to those suffering from right neglect, but made perfect sense to me, since I neglect only what happens on my left.

Having this type of adventure every weekday morning helped me realize the social skills my stroke had left me with could use some fine tuning. However, given the lack of skills I observed in my classmates, I also realized I have nothing to complain about. This half hour of rec therapy exercised both my mental and physical skills, and provided a smooth segue between PT and my attention/concentration/memory session.

Apparently my inability to pay attention to anything for more than a minute or two was painfully obvious to my rehab team. To lengthen my attention span, a therapist would take me and a few patients with similar cognitive challenges to a distracting area and give us an assignment which challenged our ability to pay attention and concentrate. Sometimes we'd play a game that required us to keep track of details. Other times we'd have to read something and then compose a summary.

Kids who try to do their homework in front of the TV provide a convenient idiom for these sessions. Somehow, their eyes and ears get sucked into the TV set as if it were a black hole. Any homework completed in front of the *tube* probably doesn't qualify as the kid's best efforts. The main benefit of my time in these therapy sessions was realizing that I, like most brain injury survivors, am very easily distracted. Fortunately, our therapist shared some tips for retaining our train of thought when our attention was drawn to something off-topic.

For example, she taught us to always make a list before going to the grocery store. Equally important, she taught us to have a plan for remembering to take the list with us. As an added bonus, she shared some handy tips for remembering a few things for a short period of time. Sometimes the first letter of each item on a list can be used to form a word that serves as a reminder. For example, if I need **b**read, **m**ilk, and eggs **w**hites from the store, I remember I'm going to the store to get *a BMW.*

Much like my time in rec therapy, the attention/concentration/ memory sessions helped me appreciate the challenges I don't face as a result of my stroke. While in rehab, I met some truly amazing people who had no idea they even had a brain injury, let alone how their brain injury had changed them or what their life would be like after leaving the hospital.

It was along about this time I began to realize the incredible blessing God had provided when I met Troy at the altar back in 1991. He was with me at least part of each of my 78 days in the hospital. So many of the patients I met never had even a single visitor. Many others saw only casual friends who, shocked by what had become of them, visited only once.

In contrast, Troy took time to visit me every day. He also continued working and managing the home-front—caring for our two young sons, paying our bills, keeping our home in order, caring for our three cats, etc. He even evaluated our options for moving forward based on how much I did/didn't recover. Troy would also get updates from my therapists when he visited so he could get their perspective on how things were going. During a visit in early March, my speech therapist mentioned I'd been falling asleep in class, which surprised her since I'd initially been highly motivated and eager to improve.

That evening, Troy noticed I seemed more tired than usual, and mentioned his concern to my nurses and rehab doctor. A key benefit of staying in the rehab area was 24/7 access to Dr. Denny, my rehab doctor. He agreed something unusual was going on and ordered some tests. The notes from Mom's journal echo their concerns:

March 2
Not much change, walked, fed herself some. Very short-term mixed up.

March 3
Less responsive.

Saturday, March 4
Less responsive. Dr. decided to put in shunt on Monday.

March 5

Slept a lot, less responsive.

My friend Helen also noticed a change about this time. She says, "Once when I came to see you, you didn't know me and your eyes were way back in your head. I was more frightened than ever for you."

An MRI showed I had developed hydrocephalus. This life-threatening medical condition is often called *water on the brain* and is usually associated with new-born babies. If left untreated for too long, hydrocephalus can apply enough pressure to the brain that it ruptures, resulting in death...obviously. Hydrocephalus can occur at any age, when too much cerebral spinal fluid (CSF) accumulates inside the skull. In my case, the CSF build-up was caused by scar tissue in the right ventricle where my right middle cerebral artery had ruptured.

Dr. Denny's note in my medical record says:

"Subsequently she developed increasing lethargy requiring placement of a ventriculoperitoneal (VP) shunt."

Troy says watching this lethargy increase was like seeing the battery that *powered* me gradually be drained of energy.

A VP shunt is a slender, flexible plastic tube that serves as a gutter, leading from the affected ventricle of the brain to a spot in the upper abdomen, midway between the breastbone and belly button.

My head was shaved, yet again, in preparation for my second brain surgery on March 7. My VP shunt was placed by none other than Dr. Carl, the neurosurgeon who'd saved my life with the emergency ventriculostomy mentioned earlier. He apparently mentioned during a family consultation about my condition that he'd put a shunt in if they wanted him to but it wouldn't make any difference. In his opinion, I'd never get out bed again if I survived.

My family knew I'd want that shot at living, no matter how remote my chances, and asked Dr. Carl to insert the shunt.

Apparently, I reacted negatively to the anesthetic used for this surgery and spent three hours vomiting in the recovery room. You know how hurling makes your head hurt? When I think of doing that for three hours, beginning right after someone drilled a hole in my skull, it almost makes me ill again. These notes from Mom's journal provide some additional insight on this period of time:

March 6
Put in shunt, shaved head

March 7
More responsive

March 8
Very talkative

March 9
Walked 120 steps very responsive

March 10
Responsive

March 14
Started group therapy

March 16
Catheter and stomach staples taken out. Sinus headache

March 17, 18, 19
Responsive and good in therapy

March 20
Started ST memory therapy.

Mentioning my shunt provides a way to open a conversation about stroke, a topic I'm eager to discuss with anyone who'll listen. Telling others about my stroke provides an easy segue to explaining how God used my stroke to guide me toward getting reconnected with Him. It never hurts to plant a seed of knowledge about how much our Heavenly Father loves us in the mind of someone who's still disconnected from Him by sin.

If Troy hadn't been monitoring my progress in therapy so closely, I might have died from hydrocephalus. Thanks to his watchful eye and Dr. Carl's steady hand, I awoke on March 8 reenergized and ready to participate in therapy. Helen saw me that day and says, "You were more yourself than I had seen you be in a long time. You knew who I was. Getting rid of the pressure on the brain was a wonderful thing. It was like a miracle to see you so much better."

Not bad for a small chunk of plastic, huh? Things clicked along pretty well for about three weeks and then I started slowing down again. Tests revealed my VP shunt needed to be tweaked a bit so Dr. Carl went back in and got things in full working order.

For some unknown reason, the person in charge of shaving my head that time elected to shave only the right side, which Dr. Carl would see. As a result, the hair on the left side of my head had a 3-week head start over the hair on my right. My trendy, new hairstyle prompted Troy to visit the cancer wing in the hospital and buy a couple of the caps often worn by those undergoing chemotherapy. It was almost seven years later when I got the opportunity to ask Dr. Carl why in the world the shaver didn't just give me a mohawk, instead of shaving only the right side. He chuckled, letting me know he appreciated my dark sense of humor.

This surgery was my final big adventure in the hospital and equipped me to stay awake in speech therapy. Communication is my strongest God-given skill so it surprises me I started dozing off in those sessions. Perhaps that's because I had to pay close attention in the sessions focused on rebuilding skills I hadn't been too good at pre-stroke. Speech was, if you'll excuse the expression, a *no-brainer* for me so I may have felt safe sleeping in those sessions.

What I didn't realize during my in-patient rehab, or for several more years, is that learning to speak is a whole different challenge than learning to shut-up. Said another way, speaking clearly and coherently is one thing, but when you add concisely to the mix, things get challenging.

Bev, my speech-language pathologist, and I worked on improving my communication skills from 10:30–11 a.m. (M-F). The recovery of my communication skills is described later but I'll tell you now what Bev had my class do after each session. She'd accompany us to lunch and sit right there while we ate. Her presence was critical because many stroke survivors struggle with dysphasia, a challenge which makes it difficult to eat safely.

Dysphasia makes it particularly difficult to safely consume liquids. Many brain injury survivors tend to accidentally inhale liquids rather than swallowing them. As a result, straws weren't allowed anywhere in the dining area. Although I was cleared of dysphasia early, I still avoid doing anything else while eating, because food and drink tend to go down the *wrong pipe*, especially if I'm overly tired or getting sick.

To help those struggling with dysphasia, the staff would add a flavorless, colorless substance to their drinks to make it *gloppy*. After this stuff is added to a liquid, the survivor can eat it instead of drinking it. (You can even make milk gloppy, although that sounds rather gross...) These lunches were terrifying for me. Although I don't suffer from dysphasia, many of those around me did and I was constantly thinking someone at my table might choke and die.

Although the nurses and therapists were vigilant about bite sizes and counting our chews, they'd often catch someone accidentally storing food in a cheek rather than swallowing it, which was called *pocketing*. Some patients would try to eat too quickly. Never a meal went by without someone inhaling food or drink, but that's how we learned. Besides, qualified medical professionals were poised to do the Heimlich maneuver, if needed.

To this day, I avoid drinking with a straw and try to eat or drink only when rested and feeling well. It's also important for me to focus only on eating at mealtimes. Although I don't (technically) have dysphasia, the left half of my tongue and throat are basically numb and I've aspirated my fair share of food and drink post-stroke.

After lunch I'd trundle off for an hour of Occupational Therapy

(OT). Contrary to the name, OT has nothing to do with employment skills. OT helps a brain injury survivor master Activities of Daily Living (ADLs). These are things most adults want to be able to do independently, such as brush teeth, comb hair, toileting, and getting dressed. You get the picture. Many of these tasks are very challenging if only half your body is on speaking terms with your brain.

Since my brain and body decided it was okay to be chummy, I was able to master all my ADLs, with one exception — TED hose. These specialized support hose have as much in common with **real** hose as a gait belt does with a **real** belt. Basically, TED hose are *girdles* for the legs, which fit about as tightly as the corset Scarlet O'Hara wore in *Gone With the Wind*. Key differences include the fact each leg gets its own *corset* and TED hose are put on by brute force. There aren't handy fasteners on the back of the leg for a helper to hook.

These handy accessories have apparently prevented thousands of ischemic (clot-related) strokes. Therefore, those who've had a stroke, as well as many aging adults, are advised to wear them. Apparently the pressure on the legs somehow prevents clots. I don't understand the medical logic behind TED hose, but soon formed the opinion they must have been designed by Satan's evil twin. I needed help donning them the whole time I was required to wear them.

My best OT learnings involved safety. For example, I learned some good safety tips in our mock cooking session. Something was obviously amiss in that class when I saw a fork protruding from the toaster in our mock kitchen... Hot forks aren't the only hazard to cooking with brain injury. (More on that later.)

At my final OT session, I proudly announced to my OT I'd put my bra on like an adult for the first time since my stroke. When she asked what I meant by that I explained I'd hooked it behind me after wrapping it around my chest. I should have shut-up at that point, but no, I went on to say, "Until this morning I had to put it on like a junior high girl, where you hook it in the front, spin it around, put your arms through the straps, and then haul it up." My OT let me know that's how she **still** puts her bra on. Oops. We probably didn't really need to know that much about each other, now did we?

My grueling work at mastering ADLs was *rewarded* with another hour of PT from 2 — 3 each afternoon.

Jenna also led self-awareness, from 3 – 3:30 each day. These sessions had a lot in common with OT, with Jenna explaining which parts of my brain no longer worked the way they used to, how that might impact my life, and how I could thrive in spite of those limitations.

These sessions were the most helpful ones for me because they were specific to me and my life. In fact, Jenna's one-page summary of why anyone with a brain injury should never, ever consume alcohol again is still safely stowed in our filing cabinet. Other topics we covered are described later.

I'll credit Jenna with making one of the few distinct memories I have from my in-patient rehab time. She's the therapist who used to greet me with a friendly, "How are you, E?" before each session. Then, after a dramatic pause, she's say, "You're probably thinking **who** are you, right?"

My daily therapy schedule concluded each day with a return trip to the dining area to eat supper with the dysphasia group. Not exactly a calming way end to the day but at least no one choked to death during my eight weeks of in-patient rehab. My therapists there helped me regain many of the skills my stroke had taken away. In fact, I got so much better that one day Troy told me I got to go home and might be moving to a rehabilitation center.

I was speechless! I finally got to go home? Troy read my misinterpretation and quickly explained my doctors had decided I was ready for a day visit to our home and that, depending on how that visit went, I might be ready to be discharged and continue my therapy elsewhere. I'd never heard of the post-acute brain injury rehabilitation center he mentioned even though it's located not far from my hometown.

The week leading up to tax day (April 15) is stressful for most Americans but it had a distinctly different type of stress for me in 2000. For starters, I found out on Thursday, April 13, I'd had a massive stroke. The next day, Troy arrived at my bedside with an entourage of medical people to tell me more about my upcoming move to a brain injury rehab center (the Center).

The hospital staff wanted to be sure Troy and I understood that my visit home was a big step forward. Thank God they were there to help us prepare for the experience, because I was still pretty wobbly on my feet. Many of the medical folks were openly referring to me as a miracle by then, and I don't think any of them wanted to see me have a set-back.

Since our home is a 4-level split, I'd have to navigate some steps during my visit. I optimistically told them the good 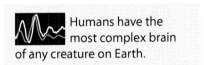 Humans have the most complex brain of any creature on Earth. news about our home is that if I wiped out on the steps, I wouldn't have far to fall. Remember? We have three sets of steps: 7, 7, and 5. One of those sets would really hurt though because it ends on the cement floor of our basement.

Being medical folks, they saw no humor in my review of our stairs and politely told Troy I'd need to wear my gait belt the *whole* time I was out of the hospital. They also reminded us of some vision deficits I have that could affect my safety. Namely, my lack of depth perception put me risk of walking into things that were in plain sight but not in my direct line of vision. The staff seemed particularly worried about my tripping over one of our sons or cats since they're pretty low to the ground. They even asked Troy if he'd have anyone there to help him keep things under control.

He optimistically assured them he'd pick me up after my Saturday morning therapy sessions, we'd all be fine, and I'd be back in time for supper. This *curfew* had nothing to do with me longing for hospital food or skipping a meal with my dysphasic friends. It was all about how health insurance providers get a bit suspicious if a hospitalized patient is well enough to spend a full day at home. Hey. When they're footing most of the bill, you play by their rules.

Troy was also informed he'd need to provide a full report of how our day went when we returned. Full report? Careful what you ask for. Clearly they hadn't realized the man doesn't overlook details.

Despite their enthusiasm about how much progress I'd made and how much I'd benefit from my time at the Center, my upcoming move didn't exactly prompt me to do cartwheels. I wanted to move back home, not to some place I'd never heard of before that sounded like a half-way house. Somehow I couldn't convince them I was ready to move home so I decided going to the Center was a good compromise for all involved. It beat staying in the hospital, and besides, change is good, right?

I must say, my first visit home was but a blur. While it's still challenging for me to focus and pay attention in unusual situations, I imagine riding in a car after being hospitalized for 11 weeks destroyed any possibility I'd remember the visit. One clear memory I do have is that all my men (Troy, Trent, and Don) came to fetch me from the hospital. After riding to the hospital's front door in a wheelchair, I walked to Troy's car using only his arm for support.

Can you believe he didn't let me drive? (As if not having my driver's license was a problem.) So I *let* Troy drive me home and, you know, the world flies by pretty quickly when you're used to staring at it through a hospital window. We made it home in what seemed a heartbeat, and Troy ushered the boys and me inside. We'd been home maybe five minutes when I met my first real challenge. Trent said, "Hey, Mom? What's for lunch?" I told him we'd eat whatever the nurses brought us. When Trent politely pointed out we don't have nurses at home, I asked him what he likes to eat. He said, "Let's just have mac and cheese, Mom." When I asked him if we had any of that, he said there was some in the pantry.

Pantry? "Hey, Troy, a little help?" I said. Troy saved the day again, as he'd done so many times the previous three months, and whipped up a lunch for our sons.

Troy dropped me off at the hospital in time for supper so I made curfew. Oddly enough, this was the first time I complained about the food. The kind-hearted nurse seated with the dysphasia group *reminded* me that evening I was always welcome to order food from the public cafeteria downstairs if the menu items didn't appeal to me. When I pointed out no one had ever told me that was an option, she suggested it might have slipped my mind.

Oh. On Day 73 of a 78-day stay, she tells me I could have been ordering *real* food the whole time. As it was, I'd been required to drink a meal-replacement drink in place of any meal I found inedible. Apparently the medical folks had been worried about my losing too much weight. When I told the nurse, the disgusting vanilla shakes I'd been having made even hospital food look edible, she pointed out the shakes come in a variety of flavors and I could have been picking those for myself, too.

All of this was too much information for a patient in the final days of a very, very long hospital stay. Oh the pleasures I'd missed simply because I didn't have both oars in the water. What a day! Needless to say, I was ready for bed after supper. My final two days in the hospital were filled with discharge meetings, admission discussions, therapy wrap-up sessions, and long-awaited farewells.

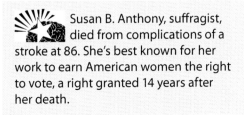 Susan B. Anthony, suffragist, died from complications of a stroke at 86. She's best known for her work to earn American women the right to vote, a right granted 14 years after her death.

CHAPTER 7

RENEWING MY MIND
WITH GOD

The hospital staff had gotten to know me well during our 11+ weeks together. That familiarity came in handy when I insisted I didn't need to go to the post-acute brain injury rehabilitation center (the Center) Troy had selected. My long-term memory told me life in our home was well-planned and carefully controlled. It also told me that since I'd personally held most of that control pre-stroke, I was ready to move home.

I didn't know why people were making such a big deal out of my *deficits*—whatever those were. There wasn't much *wrong* with me, as far as I knew, and thought Troy could help me relearn things better than a bunch of strangers. What I didn't know was that my visit home had been very stressful for him. Troy had told my friend, Kari, he "really had his hands full" looking out for both our sons and me, and that visit had lasted only a few hours.

The staff members were the only ones who knew, at that time, my stroke had left me rather impulsive. Based on their experience working with brain-injury survivors, they knew my

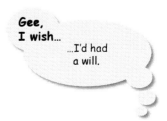

Gee, I wish...
...I'd had a will.

time at the Center would help me relearn some restraint.

Problem was, I hadn't yet realized stroke had ripped most of the (perceived) control I had in my life from my hands. Much like Max Pruss, captain of the Hindenburg, something unexpected and very, very bad had happened aboard my *ship*. The next thing I knew... BOOM! Life as I knew it no longer existed. Like Captain Pruss I survived the initial crash and had the opportunity to salvage something from the wreckage.

Although going to the Center sounded like a waste of time to me, Troy wrapped up the details behind my transfer the morning of April 18. He then promised to pick me up over his lunch hour and headed to work. I was waiting in a wheelchair at the front door, my belongings strewn on a cart, when he arrived. Troy piled my stuff in the trunk, helped me into the passenger's seat, secured my seatbelt, and we headed out. I must say, it's a fine deal to arrive at a hospital by ambulance and leave by car.

Our ride was—in a word—**terrifying**. I immediately missed the security of the hospital and dreaded staying at the Center. Besides, Troy seemed to be driving really fast. He was probably only going about 65 miles per hour but it may as well have been the speed of light. My rides a few days earlier hadn't bothered me nearly as much as that one did. What a difference a few days can make when one's brain is getting itself back in gear.

Troy was fairly quiet while driving, as usual. He did, however, take the opportunity to tell me something he hadn't felt comfortable sharing at the hospital. Troy assured me that when we'd recited our marriage vows nine years earlier, he'd meant it when he promised to love, honor, and cherish me, **in sickness** and in health. I've never questioned whether Troy meant what he said, because he's a man of his word, but his willingness to stay at my side post-stroke has been a true test of that vow.

Neither of us had any idea Troy's words would be put to the test so severely, or so soon, when we made that promise to one another. Most marriages don't survive the challenges that surface when one spouse becomes a stroke survivor. The example Troy is setting for our sons and me, is one I'd do my best to duplicate for him, if need be. You can be sure God hears me express my gratitude each day for this wonderful man at my side.

After a brief conversation with Katy, the Center's admissions person, Troy completed some paperwork and returned to work, assuring me he'd stop by later. As Katy walked me to my room, I noticed some unusual décor around the Center. For example, the walls by the front entrance were painted with brightly colored cartoon-like figures. Katy answered my unasked question, saying some of the early *clients* had painted the walls as part of their occupational therapy (OT).

Oddly enough, I also noticed each hallway we passed was painted a different color. I say *oddly* because it amazes me I noticed something with my eyes. Katy quickly explained how the color scheme helps clients with orientation problems find their way around. She then said my room was at the end of the green hallway. I had the *pole position* in the hallway of my favorite color. April 18 was shaping up pretty well, after all!

About then I noticed a small whiteboard near the nurses' station which said something akin to, "Today is April 18, 2000. You are staying in TOWN. The weather outside is sunny but cool." Katy said  For some reason, the number 14 usually slips out in conversation when I need to say a random number. For example, "I can only do 14 things at a time." some of the clients there struggle with time and spatial orientation and the whiteboard helps them get their bearings each day.

Katy kept using the word *client* as we walked, so I asked what that meant. She explained that those served at the Center are referred to as clients because *patients* are generally hospitalized. As a *words person*, I appreciated that difference immediately. I now know the word *client* appealed to me because being a *patient* made me feel like a victim, and I didn't want to be one of those. A victim is powerless and must passively submit to those *in-power*.

A *survivor* is the opposite of a *victim* because she plays some role in what becomes of her life. Anyone who maintains a personal relationship with Jesus Christ is a survivor because that relationship connects her with God. This connection gives a saved person 24/7 access to God because His Holy Spirit dwells in her and is in constant conversation with Him, on her behalf. Romans 8:26 tells us, "...we know not what we should pray for as we ought: but the Spirit itself maketh intercession for us with groanings which cannot be uttered."

Conversely, anyone going through this life separated from God by sin is living as a *victim*. Without the influence of God's Holy Spirit, a person is left *wide-open* to Satan's temptations. If that description piques your curiosity, please read the *Epilogue* now. Just be sure to return to this page when you're done.

As we toured, I found-out I was expected to wear *normal* clothes (sweatpants, T-shirt, and tennis shoes) at the Center. This was a huge improvement over the hospital gowns I'd worn for months but also meant I'd need to find someone to do my laundry. Although I was sure Troy would be willing to do that for me, I dreaded asking him. He'd already done—and was doing—so much for our family.

> This arrangement reminded me of visiting my parents while in college. Mom knew a mountain of laundry awaited her in the trunk, whenever I pulled in their drive.

My parents used to remind me there's always someone who has it worse than me and my time in the Center showed me their wisdom certainly applies to brain injury. I may walk a bit robotically and struggle to keep my mouth shut but most of the clients I met face far bigger challenges.

Each of the 20+ clients at the Center was working to rebuild connections between their injured brain and their body. Some were relearning to walk; others lacked a sense of personal identity. Several clients were partially paralyzed. Some, including me, were trying to piece-together what had happened to them.

I couldn't help but wonder why God would let something as terrible as brain injury happen to anyone. Had these people ticked Him off so badly they were being punished? Why had it happened to me? Had I done something to deserve this? After all, humans are God's most beloved creation, so why'd He even create brain injury?

My time at the Center didn't help me find answers to these questions but it sure got me thinking. Neither my heart nor mind was ready for the answers at that time, anyway. Interacting with other brain injury survivors also pushed me to start wondering, "What's next, Lord?" Although I pondered that question while at the Center, I didn't ask Him.

> **SideNote:** God helped me find my own answer to that question, years later. I now believe terrors such as cancer, tsunamis, starvation, stroke, drought, etc. are the end result of people living without the light of Jesus Christ in their life. Said another way, every person who isn't yet saved has no true defense against Satan's temptations. Based on how people often treat one another, I'd say Satan is getting his way quite often. The sins committed since Adam and Eve broke God's one rule in the Garden of Eden have contributed to the condition of this world.

Katy also introduced me to several of the therapists I'd begin working with the next day. The *agenda* she gave me listed all sorts of fun and adventures the staff had planned for me during my seven weeks at the Center. They had every Monday through Friday booked solid for me from just after breakfast until bedtime.

My agenda was based on input from Troy and the therapists I'd worked with in the hospital. It accurately reflected how stroke had affected me and supported the staff's goal of *rebuilding* me as much as possible during my stay. That was an aggressive and laudable goal, for that stage of my recovery.

My sole focus was to be on regaining abilities I'd lost. Regaining or rebuilding identifiable skills strikes me as a reasonable goal, for someone in therapy at a place like the Center. In retrospect, however, this before-and-after (stroke) view of my abilities put my life on hold for about six years.

The staff's agenda reminds me of the difference between completing a paint-by-number scene and painting a picture freehand.

The staff knew what skills I needed to relearn and had an image for how I'd *turn-out*. I hadn't yet realized God was waiting for me to become a completely different person than I'd been pre-stroke so I went along with the staff's plan. Besides, all the skills they planned to help me relearn are vital in this world.

The saying, "comparisons are nothing but hurtful"—a reminder I periodically give our sons—came to mind as I scanned my agenda. It seemed there was more *wrong* with me that needed to be *fixed* than I'd noticed on my own.

About now, an overwhelming sense of gratitude started brewing in my heart. I'd survived a brain hemorrhage and massive stroke. I'd beaten the ten percent chance of living my doctors afforded me. My arm and leg were back on speaking terms with my brain and I could speak clearly, if not concisely. My loving family anxiously awaited my return home. I was getting a bit better each day and have the rest of my life to keep improving. What did I have to complain about? Nothing.

> **SideNote:** If you're one of those folks who question the need for motorcycle and bike helmets, please consider visiting a brain injury rehab center. Many of the clients I met at the Center had sustained a traumatic brain injury when they wiped out on a 2-wheeler without a helmet. To me, wearing a helmet sends a message to others that you value your life and understand you're mortal. Your body is a temple *on loan* from God which provides a temporary home for your soul and His Holy Spirit. When you die, your temple falls, your soul moves on to spend eternity elsewhere, and God's Holy Spirit lives on within other saved people. I became one of those saved people when I accepted Jesus Christ as my personal Lord and Savior. As a result, Heaven is my soul's final destination. Hope to see you there.

In my quest to reassemble my mind, I participated in PT, OT, speech, and recreational therapy sessions while at the Center. These sessions focused on helping me overcome the same losses targeted by my therapists in the hospital, but incorporated activities much more representative of real life.

One PT stunt I repeated time and again while there involved bouncing on a large rubber ball. My physical therapist, Roy, convinced me to sit atop a 3-foot wide ball and gently bounce, explaining it would stimulate my vestibular nervous system. When I asked if I have that type of system and, if so, how bouncing could possibly be good for it, he said every human has a vestibular nervous system and bouncing on a big ball would help improve how mine was working.

He then explained that this system helps us perceive how and where our body is positioned in space and how it's moving. Given I frequently lost track of the left side of my body, that made sense. My balance was **really** bad at the time and if bouncing on a big ball would help me avoid walking into doorways, poles, and other people, I was all for it.

So, I took my life into my hands, yet again, and perched myself on the ball. The first several bounces were unnerving but I knew I'd have a soft landing if I wiped-out because the floor was covered with cushioned mats. (The first time Troy saw me perform this daring feat, he seemed to be more taken by the fact he'd graduated from high school with my therapist.)

More adventures awaited me in speech therapy. My ability to speak clearly had returned pretty quickly, so Denae, my new speech therapist, decided to concentrate on improving my writing skills. My ability to write clearly, concisely, and quickly had helped me earn rapid advancements in my job pre-stroke. When Denae and I discussed how my stroke **might** have affected my writing skills, I was terrified! What if she was right? What if my finely tuned writing abilities had gotten zapped? What if I now wrote like I spoke? She had the perfect *what-if* for me. "What if you put off finding out how your writing was affected until you return to work?"

When she put it that way, I decided maybe the Center was a better place to come to terms with whatever **might** have happened to my writing skills. It's generally helpful to be aware of a problem before it makes itself apparent. To that end, Denae gave me an *easy* writing assignment, with two goals: write a letter about my stroke experience and mail it to an appropriate group of people.

She knew this assignment required me to draw on skills that are near and dear to my heart. God gifted me with the ability to write clearly and I'd nurtured that skill through my education and career. She also knew these skills are dependent on some areas of my brain which had gotten *reorganized*. Denae added a goal—a mail-by date—when I'd made no progress a week later. She must have known I was churning the same information about my stroke over and over in my mind. Denae also decided to help me with the first step—developing an outline—which took all the mental energy I could muster.

Writing down what I'd been hearing about my stroke prompted the reality of my situation to take root. It also required Denae to gather more information from my medical record so I could write an accurate summary. Fortunately, she recognizes when a client's emotions are getting the best of her and often advised me to take a mental break. I wrote my first draft of the letter after Denae and I were comfortable with the outline.

For me, a huge benefit of computers I realized post-stroke, is the ease with which I can capture random thoughts, save what I've written, and then rearrange my thoughts online. If I'd written my update letter in pen on notebook paper, I would definitely not have met Denae's mail-by date. As it was, I had to rely on her to tell me to stop rearranging words and get my letter mailed. It turned out pretty well but my diminished ability to select an appropriate audience came into play when I mailed it to everyone on my Christmas card list, plus several colleagues.

Writing that letter prompted a painful collision between my pre- and post-stroke 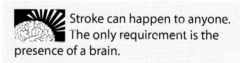 Stroke can happen to anyone. The only requirement is the presence of a brain. communication abilities, but what I learned from Denae provided the foundation needed to write this book.

Some of my cognitive losses appeared in other therapy sessions. For example, Roy helped me identify one in PT. After I began walking pretty well, Roy, never one to leave well enough alone, raised the bar by saying he thought I was ready for the bike. The first few times Roy said that, I pretended I didn't hear him because I knew my balance wasn't good enough to ride a bike. That old saying about never forgetting how to ride a bike may be true but has nothing to do with whether or not you can ride one without accidentally killing yourself.

When I arrived for PT one afternoon, Roy told me I was **going to** ride the bike that day. The time for subtle hints was obviously gone so I asked the question that had been haunting me. "Do you have a helmet I can wear?" Common sense told me that if Roy believed I could ride a bike safely and he had a helmet I could wear, I should give it a try.

He looked dumbfounded and said, "Why in the world would you need a helmet to ride a stationary bike?" Talk about feeling like a mental midget... Here I'd been thinking he wanted me to take a 2-wheeler around town. The best response I could come up with was, "Better safe than sorry." Roy probably knew I'd misinterpreted his comments about bikes but let it go and followed me to the stationary bike without comment.

After thinking on this disconnect for a while, I realized I'd interpreted his comments about bike riding very literally and had formed an opinion based on my long-term memory. Prior to my stroke, I relied on current information to form opinions and thought rather abstractly. My long-term memories of bike riding were of a bike that moved forward when I pedaled.

Realizing Roy wanted me to ride a stationary bike required me to *think outside the box*, something that's not automatic for my injured brain.

Something similar happened when I called my friend, Jack, from the Center to let him know what was going on. Jack and I hadn't talked for ages but I recalled his phone number without looking it up. When he answered the phone, he first asked if I was calling from home or work, I said, "Neither; I'm calling from a rehab center." His response of, "Did you get in some trouble with drugs, E?" left me speechless.

Jack had known me since I was 16 and knew full-well I'd never use an illegal drug. After explaining I was staying in a post-acute brain injury rehab center, he said, "Were you in an accident?" It hadn't crossed my mind until then that many people don't realize brain injury is often caused by stroke, and that healthy, active, young women can have a stroke. The most gratifying part of our conversation, as he pointed out, was the simple fact I'd thought to call him.

One thing that frustrated me about therapy, both at the hospital and the Center, was that it was so hard for me to notice my progress. Trying to spot incremental improvements in skills which used to be automatic has a lot in common with watching one's hair grow. Although I was continually improving in therapy, it was tough to notice the differences.

My less-frequent visitors could see my improvements and were often kind enough to mention them. For example, one person pointed out I'd graduated from using a walker to a 4-pronged cane between her visits. Until she helped me look at it that way, all I saw was that I still needed a cane to walk.

A person living with brain injury is the only one positioned to truly evaluate her cognitive progress, unless she's working with a neuropsychologist. This type of psychologist specializes in identifying relationships between a person's brain and behavior. My most vivid memories of therapy at the Center are of my time with Dr. Lee, the onsite neuropsychologist. Assuming you still have all the brain cells you were born with, you probably haven't met one of these docs. I suggest you protect your grey matter and keep it that way.

My sessions with Dr. Lee were one-on-one. As a starting point, he had me complete a six-and-a-half hour neuropsychological evaluation. This quantitative measure of logic and reasoning abilities was administered over a 3-day period to accommodate my limited attention span.

After evaluating my responses, Dr. Lee and I discussed them so I'd understand more specifically how my brain injury might affect my life. Better yet, he provided suggestions for how I can thrive in spite of my cognitive losses. He also introduced me to the term *perseverate,* well-described by the saying, "Like a dog with a bone."

Once I get a notion in my mind, it's very difficult for me to switch topics or consider modifying my thought in any way.

Troy had said the staff would allow me to occasionally stay overnight at home and, as we walked, I asked Katy if the upcoming weekend was an option. She said the staff there needed to get to know my *caregiver* (Troy) and me before my first overnight visit. That kind of bummed me out because our ninth wedding anniversary would be the following week and I thought it would be wonderful to spend a day at home with Troy and the boys the prior weekend. However, I figured the staff had reasons for being cautious and didn't press the issue.

My favorite therapy sessions while at the Center were what I called *kid/cat therapy*. When the staff was confident a caregiver would ensure a client's safety, the caregiver could take the client out for a few hours, or even overnight. Needless to say, Troy met their standards easily so the staff granted my request for an overnight visit home. Troy, Trent, and Don picked me up after my Saturday morning therapy sessions on April 29.

> **SideNote:** This was the only time our sons set foot inside the Center. Apparently, they had an experience similar to one I recall from visiting a nursing home when I was a child. Some of the lonelier clients were so happy to see their bright, young faces, they reached out to touch the boys as they passed.

The thought of going home for a day was so exciting I could barely get to sleep the night before! It just seemed unreal I was going to sleep in my own bed the following night. Can you imagine the one thing on my mind when Troy and I walked into our home the next morning? What would any young woman who'd been living away from home for three months want to do?

Take a bubble bath, of course! After three months of sponge baths and assisted showers, I was ready for a long soak in warm bubbles. Somehow life just seems more bearable when viewed from a vantage point below the edge of a bubbly tub.

When I told Troy I was going to take a bath, he said, "Okay. You can shut the door if you want, but don't lock it." This should have been my first clue Troy felt he needed to be more protective of me than he'd been in the past, and rightfully so.

His response made no sense to me at the time but I complied. Anything for a bubble bath. My bathroom, decorated exactly as I wanted, looked just as I remembered. What a relief. One shock was the poster I'd hung in the room years earlier which shows a girl carrying a knapsack who's reached a fork in the road. The two paths she can choose are labeled "Your Life" and "No Longer an Option." This image has been my favorite since I was in college but now seemed all too relevant, as I realized how stroke had forced me to take a path full of new adventures.

Falling asleep next to Troy that evening was surely the closest I'll get to Heaven in this lifetime. Waking up the next morning was a bit of a shock, however, because I heard a voice saying something akin to, "Come here you little, *Pucker*. Over here *Pucky*-Duck." Was that Trent I heard? Where had he learned those words? What had been going on around home in my absence?

After hearing these obscenities repeated, I woke Troy up and asked him why Trent was saying that. He seemed to think it was no big deal and said Trent sometimes mispronounced Puck's name. "Who in the world is Puck?" I asked in disbelief. Troy said, "Oh you remember Puck, the black and white cat you and Trent got at the humane society not long before your stroke?"

I didn't remember getting a black and white cat and I certainly wouldn't have knowingly named her Puck at the time Don was just learning to speak. That's way too dangerous — mispronunciations do happen, you know. I walked cautiously to the kitchen and saw Trent on his hands and knees saying very clearly, "Come here you little *Pucker*."

My first cognitive challenge of the day came when I realized I couldn't tell him not to say that word, which closely resembles *Pucker*, because then I'd have to explain it and he'd be tempted to say it intentionally. God provided the words I needed and I told Trent, "You need to be very careful to say Puck's name the same way as Dad and Mom because if you put the F sound in front of it, it makes a very inappropriate word."

Apparently the look on my face convinced the lad I was serious because he said, "Sorry Mom." Then I asked Trent where Puck had come from and how she got her name. He reminded me we'd picked her out in November of 1999, shortly after my beloved cat, George, died. Puck had been two at the time and was living with a name that just didn't match our other kitty's name, Ping.

As Trent filled me in, Troy shoved a picture in my face showing Trent, next to Puck on a cat perch at the humane society, and the memories came flooding back. I looked at Trent and said, "Oh that's right. I let you pick a good name for her when we brought her home. She jumped out of her carrier and started running around so you said, 'Look Mom! She's little and she's black and she moves really fast on the floor, just like a hockey puck. Let's call her Puck!"

My second real cognitive challenge hit after lunch when Trent asked, "Hey, Mom? Why'd you even have to go to the hospital?" That should've been an easy question for me to answer, right? So I started talking. Of course I had no idea, at that time, what had actually happened to me but that didn't stop me from explaining everything to him as well as I could.

Three hours later—yes, you read that correctly, three **hours** later—Troy interrupted me to say it was time to head back to the Center. I don't know if Trent learned anything from my blathering, but I did. It was the first time I realized my verbal abilities seemed less reliable than they'd once been.

My family picked me up at the Center after my Saturday morning therapy sessions each of the following five weeks. These overnight *visits* home helped me see and prepare for what life would be like when I moved home. Gradually, I realized the expectations of a wife and mother are quite different from those of a patient or client.

Home was quite intimidating during my first visit. I hadn't anticipated that reaction, but couldn't deny it: I actually missed the Center. All of the clients there could relate to my feelings of inadequacy and fear, because each of us was learning to live with brain injury. That's when I began to realize moving home would be frightening. However, I also realized I'd never again be alone on my life's journey. I could feel God's presence as He took each step with me. Although I missed the security of the Center during these visits, I talked of nothing but my *kid/cat therapy* when I returned there each Sunday afternoon.

The therapists at the Center sometimes team-up to help clients rebuild their social skills through community outings. During my time there, I participated in an outing planned by the staff and one I planned myself. The staff-planned outing, a trip to watch a minor league baseball game, was one I'd unwittingly observed in the past.

Troy and I used to go watch this AAA baseball team play quite often and would occasionally notice a group of fans in wheelchairs. Suddenly in April of 2000, I found myself sitting among that very group. Granted, the faces were different from those I'd seen before but there I was, sitting with a group of fans with special needs. It was exciting to do something I recalled from my pre-stroke life, but also a tad embarrassing to be *glumped* in with a bunch of people who have a brain injury. Oh, that's right—I was one of them now, wasn't I?

My second community outing wasn't just fun and games. Before being released from the Center, I had to demonstrate I could think-up a community event, do the necessary planning, and then participate in it. After talking with Troy, I decided to arrange a photo appointment for our sons at a local store. This outing involved me finding the studio's phone number; picking a time that worked for Troy, the boys, and me; and then calling the store to schedule a setting. I also had to decide what I wanted the boys to wear and pass that information along to Troy so he'd have them dressed appropriately that day.

Our plan was for Troy and the boys to pick me up at the Center that morning on the way to the store. Everything went as planned and I passed my *final exam*.

My seven weeks at the rehab center were time well spent. Those who'd convinced me to move there with an open mind had known

I'd benefit greatly from being around other brain injury survivors who'd chosen to make the best of their situation, rather than view themselves as *victims*. Each client I met there faces life with a unique set of challenges but all share two key traits: loss of control over their life and the will to live. My heart was filled with gratitude for what I'd learned and seen at the Center when I left.

When I walked—unassisted—into our home on June 2, my life was very different than the one I'd left behind four months earlier. The three people I love most—Troy, Trent, and Don—were still at my side though and a new love had entered my life, an all-consuming love for our Heavenly Father. Although He's been with me since before I was even born (Psalms 139:13-18) it took a major *boot to the head* for me to recognize His eternal presence.

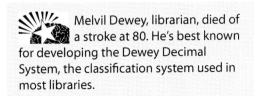

Melvil Dewey, librarian, died of a stroke at 80. He's best known for developing the Dewey Decimal System, the classification system used in most libraries.

CHAPTER 8

THERE'S NO PLACE
LIKE HOME

I'd expected perfection of myself from an early age and had grown accustomed to being in control of attaining that perfection. I unrealistically thought I was still *in control* and should be able to dive back into my former roles without a hitch when I got home.

It might have simplified things a bit if my therapists had simply told Troy and me <u>everything</u> in our relationship would be different when I moved home. Hearing a medical professional tell us it would be perfectly *normal* for everything to *feel* different might have helped us set more realistic expectations. That insight might have prompted us to realize I might not *fit in* as well as I had before my stroke.

My move home from the Center reminds me of how a mother bird eventually pushes her babies from the nest. She knows it's time for them to fly and as each one falls through the air, it begins flapping its wings. The staff members who'd gotten to know me during my 7-week stay served as my *mother bird*, working with Troy to set my discharge

Gee, I wish... ...I'd ridden all the best roller coasters in America.

date and help ensure my move was as smooth as possible. A key difference between my move and that of a baby bird is I got kicked back into my *nest*. I was returning to a familiar place where I'd be surrounded by those who have my best interests at heart.

Troy, Trent, Don, and I were more than ready to be reunited, at the emotional level. They missed me, and I missed them. The staff at the Center knew my return home would place additional stress on our family, at the practical level, however. I could talk and walk, but my therapists had detected some cognitive deficits as we worked together. Their input reduced the stress leading up to my discharge, but no amount of planning can fully prepare a family to welcome home a stroke survivor who looks as she did before but whose thinking has been rearranged in ways no one completely understands.

To me, home is defined by physical surroundings **and** the manner in which I'm treated. Like most people, I find it comforting to be surrounded by familiar décor and my family. Staying overnight in a motel is a good reminder of how comforting it is to be home. Most folks sleep better in their own bed and start the day in a better frame of mind when they choose an outfit from their own closet. Our home is decorated in a way that suits our family's style, and I'd organized the items I used so I could quickly find them.

When I arrived home from the Center, I thought things looked just like I'd left them, 125 days before. Troy, true-to-form, had kept things in order while I was hospitalized. I was soon reminded, however, that Troy and I have polar opposite organizing styles.

> This may help explain why he once found a box of cereal in a storage box under our bed reserved for lost socks. The location had made sense to me, and Troy's need to check the box to be sure it contained only socks made sense to him. When he challenged my logic, I challenged his need to seek organizing gaffes, and then agreed to move the cereal to the pantry. When a packrat and a tidy-bug make a lifelong commitment to one another, they learn to compromise.

As I started looking around the house, I noticed things weren't really as I'd left them. Anything Troy had used had been put back where he thought it belonged. This *Troy-style* organization meant I had trouble finding lots of things. While it was gratifying to be able to remember where I'd put specific items, it was frustrating when something wasn't where I thought it belonged and I had to ask Troy where he'd put it. Troy quickly got used to my asking where I could find things and, because he's so consistent, I eventually learned to look where I thought he might have put something before asking him for help.

Also, although my memory insisted I was in charge of what happened around our home, Troy had assumed that role in my absence. This reality hit me when Trent asked, "What's for lunch, Dad?" Feeding the boys was my job, last time I checked, so why would he be asking Troy? As I walked to the kitchen to defend my territory, I noticed something amiss. There were no plants on my cupboards. When I asked Troy what he'd done with my beloved philodendrons, he said they'd died from lack of water a couple of weeks after my stroke so he'd pitched them.

Troy then explained how he'd suddenly had a lot of things to take care of and some non-essential tasks had fallen through the cracks. Now granted, philodendrons are the peons of the plant world, but I'd had those plants for years. I'd lived with them longer than I'd lived with Troy!

For some reason, the loss of these plants hit me hard and I started to cry. Okay—I sobbed. In an attempt to lighten the moment, Troy pointed out, "It's no big deal to get new plants."

He'd done his best to divide his time among working full-time, keeping our sons' lives stable, visiting and supporting me, coming to terms with the loss of the person I'd been before my stroke, and keeping our home in good order. How in the world could I be upset with him for not watering a few plants?

This type of emotional outburst had been fairly common among the clients at the Center but I seemed to be the only one in our home who cried. Troy and the boys were accustomed to me having everything, including my emotions, under control. They'd certainly never seen me cry over plants.

That's when it dawned on me why Dr. Lee had invested so much time explaining why I was so emotional, during my time in the Center. Rampant emotions can result when physical changes in the brain impact how a person handles her feelings. This annoyance seemed to run my life the first few weeks I was back at home. Things that wouldn't have fazed me pre-stroke often prompted tears or an angry outburst. I might *flood* or *snap* at the slightest provocation.

Dr. Lee had known I needed to learn to live with my new, more emotive self. This first in-home *flood* provided some early insight on how my cognitive deficits might impact others. My therapists at the Center had helped me learn how my brain injury would likely impact my life but hadn't invested much time helping me understand how others might be affected.

You can't get much practical experience about coping with the 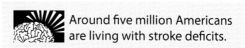 Around five million Americans are living with stroke deficits. real world while housed in a post-acute brain injury rehab center. For the most part, you have to get back into the real world to learn that. Moving back home helped me realize that when a person changes due to brain injury, everyone who cares about her is also changed, by default. The changes caused by a brain injury are usually unexpected, sudden, and trying.

The benefits of having medical professionals available to help me 24/7 became painfully obvious soon after I got home. In the hospital and the Center, someone had always been available to help keep me safe and comfortable. Now there was no call button to press when I needed or wanted help. I either had to fend for myself or recruit a *volunteer* (Troy, Trent, or Don) to help me. In addition, I quickly realized God has a call button I can press anytime. Whenever life feels a bit out-of-control, I can simply turn my thoughts to Him in prayer.

Troy took much of the responsibility for helping me make good decisions when I returned home by keeping a watchful eye on my every move. He'd been doing that for Trent and Don in my absence, and now added me to the mix.

When I used to return from a business trip, Troy could relax and

I'd take care of our sons. Single parenting is tough, even if for only a few days. My move home from the Center added stress—and lots of it—to Troy's already too-full plate. He'd taken care of everything while I was gone. Now he also had to take care of/look after me. Troy didn't know what was or wasn't safe to assume about my abilities so he erred on the side of caution. He really dislikes change but started trying to get familiar with my new *skill set* right away. Troy has taken his promise to love, honor, and cherish me for the rest of his life, very seriously from the day we wed.

When I think of the time, energy, and effort his vigilance required, I can see why so many spouses/caregivers of a stroke survivor file for divorce rather than honoring their vows in sickness and in health. *Raising* a stroke survivor is tough, often thankless, work, and there's no known completion date.

Troy's vigilance also helped protect my relationship with our sons. I learned as a child to rely on my quick thinking and verbal abilities to influence others. Moving back home brought to light the fact my stroke had slowed my thinking and diminished my verbal and social skills. These deficits are still noticeable in casual conversations but my resident cognitive therapists—Troy, Trent, and Don—provide frequent opportunities to practice improving.

For example, during a conversation with one of the boys about a video platform he wanted but couldn't afford, I started telling God why those conversations drive me crazy. Just as our son began drowning out by my conversation with God, I heard Him say, "Stop talking about video games until Troy enters the conversation as your moderator."

My willingness to speak my mind was a mixed blessing when I first moved home though. When Trent or Don said something or acted out to get my attention, there was no telling what might come out of my mouth. Troy helped corral this problem early on by being ever vigilant. This approach didn't help much when Troy was the target of one of my verbal attacks, however.

What a blessing it is God entered our home with me on June 2. Although I didn't recognize His presence that day, I now know I couldn't have handled the fear and insecurity haunting me without

Him. Troy, the boys, and I were thrilled to be reunited, and I was
so giddy with excitement I couldn't have told you if I was coming
or going. Troy's enthusiasm was, in contrast, tempered by thoughts
of the future. I'm sure it was maddening to him that no one could
tell him how much or how quickly I'd recover.

Over the ensuing seven years, I realized God's always been at
my side but I hadn't noticed His presence before my stroke. Accepting Jesus Christ as my personal Lord and Savior is my soul's
ticket to Heaven. It's also what enabled me to begin feeling God's
presence in my daily life. I began to see the world through new
eyes at this turning point in my life. Becoming a new creature
in Christ also made it impossible for me to disregard God's cues
about how I should live my life. After all, as God tells us in Psalm
139, He knows everything about us and has since long before we
were born. No one else will ever know me as well as our Heavenly
Father does.

With my God lens in place, I now choose to do only those activities which have eternal value. If the eternal value of a task, such as
housework, escapes me, a quick Internet search helps me see how
other Christians view it. If my search yields no evidence of eternal
value, I stop doing that activity.

This approach to time management has prompted me to stop
spending time on TV, alcohol, and popular music. I do occasionally sit with our sons when they watch a show but my mind is on
what they're absorbing, not on the show itself. Banning television
from my life is a blessing many times over because it:

- **Keeps unneeded information out of my mind.** Trust
  me, this is a huge benefit for my injured brain. My
  mind used to automatically sort and purge disruptive
  information. Since my stroke, if my mind absorbs this
  type of news, it rumbles around inside my cranium until I purposely decide what to do with it. To help make
  that decision, I'll read my Bible, pray, take a walk, soak
  in a bubbly bath, or if all else fails take a nap.
- **Doesn't glorify the enemy's work.** Satan often gets his
  way here on Earth but I choose to not let his little suc-

cesses affect my life. I see no point in lending credence to his work by spending time watching it or hearing about it. He may win some battles but he's gonna lose the war. For more on that, read the Book of Revelation.

- **Frees-up time to invest in activities with eternal value.** If I watch two hours of TV a day, about eight percent of my life is just gone for that day. That would significantly reduce the amount of time I could invest with God.
- **Encourages conversation.** To stay current on world events, I talk with Troy and the boys, friends, and folks at our local YMCA. If I don't hear about something from one of these sources, I probably don't need to know about it.
- **Sets an example I'll be proud for our sons to follow.** *Do as I do* seems to work much better than *do as I say.*

My stroke and subsequent return home brought to light a major role reversal for Troy and me. I'd been the primary breadwinner and caregiver in our home before my stroke. He'd assumed both roles in my absence. When I returned home, we had to figure out what roles each of us would fill, going forward. The great unknown was whether or not I could be a wife, mom, household manager, and employee again. Would it all be second nature as it had been before my stroke? Could I make and implement important decisions on my own? How frustrating it must have been for Troy that no one could answer these questions.

Predicting how well a person will recover from a brain injury is a bit like predicting how many blossoms a favorite rose bush will sport each spring. You may know the plant well, fertilize it as you should, water it carefully, prune dead twigs, and protect it from bugs, but you never know for sure how well it will bloom.

There's no way to adequately prepare someone for the responsibilities of caring for a stroke survivor at home but the therapists at the hospital and the Center helped Troy find his way. They provided suggestions, contact information, and helped him understand how he could make my transition back home easier. Stroke recovery happens one step at a time and requires lots of patience. The fact of the matter is that recovering from stroke is a lifelong journey filled with achievements and setbacks. Achievements are usually incremental; setbacks often monumental. As the Winter Warlock says in *Santa Claus is Coming to Town*, "you put one foot in front of the other."

Newborn babies all have a lot in common so they're fairly predictable. However, each stroke survivor re-enters the world with remnants of her pre-stroke self still intact. This means she has a unique set of new needs and feelings about what happened to her. As a result, Troy had his hands full when I returned home. Those who help a stroke survivor get readjusted to life in the real world are called caregivers. He'd been a caregiver to Trent and Don, with me as his co-pilot, for years.

Becoming a caregiver for one's spouse is a whole, different ballgame, however. A man can be fairly parochial with his children, but not with his opinionated, outspoken, independent wife. There doesn't seem to be a class focused on helping stroke survivors and their caregivers get back out into the world. Perhaps that's because each survivor's pre-stroke life and stroke deficits are unique to him. As a result, we couldn't immediately dive back into our rather typical marriage relationship.

My therapists must have told Troy not to let me out of his sight or to entrust me with anything considered irreplaceable. Hmmm… That guidance covers a lot of ground and requires a lot of direct supervision. In response to their suggestions, he was ever vigilant. Their guidance was affirmed early-on as I resumed some responsibilities I'd held pre-stroke, such as helping our younger son bathe.

God's answers to my prayers are clear but I often have trouble understanding what other people say to me. This may be an attention challenge.

Although I'd regained the ability to safely complete my activities of daily living, no one had a clear picture on how my stroke had impacted the cognitive abilities I needed to make safe, sound decisions on-the-fly. For example, it seems I'd forgotten it's unsafe (and unwise) to leave a 2-year-old unattended in the bathtub. Granted, it's unlikely Don would have drowned, but it was possible. Besides, I didn't really want him to use an entire bottle of bubble bath each night.

Then there was the time Troy bolted downstairs early one Saturday morning because our washing machine was making odd noises. I was shocked to see him awake and then he asked what I'd put in the washing machine. He threw the lid up to find the answer himself and gasped to see it *packed to the gills*. The motor was whining under the stress of me overloading the tub. After extracting about half of the load and telling me what I'd done wrong, Troy went back upstairs. I stood there feeling like an idiot and a failure.

Since Troy's more of a get 'er done person than a cuddly kind of guy, our sons provided much of the warmth and encouragement I so desperately needed early-on. Besides, it was difficult for Troy to get away and relax. He seemed to feel he needed to be home with the boys and me as much as possible. When Troy did manage to pull himself away, I fear he was so distracted by what was going on at home, he was unable to relax and enjoy himself.

It seems to me every married couple should attend to keeping their responsibilities well-balanced. After all, no person is exactly the same today as she was yesterday, and when she changes, everyone in a relationship with her is also changed. Because the changes (directly) affect only her mind, her mate may be rather disconcerted, especially if she's unable to help him understand what's different. One alternative is for him to observe and respond to the end results of her thinking.

These changes in our marriage made home a bit less comforting, initially. Although I've long since stopped thinking of Troy as my caregiver, he certainly was when I first moved home because I was a new, unknown person. We continue to work toward a good balance of responsibilities as he and I adjust to my new *skill set*, one which is a bit better each day. Troy may have bitten off more than he could chew when he brought me home from the rehab center, but thank God he took that leap of faith.

At least no one needed to worry about me having another stroke when I moved back home. Because my stroke was hemorrhagic, rather than ischemic, my risk of stroke is no higher today than it was pre-stroke. In my mind, I have a lower risk of stroke now than I did in 2000 because I take better care of myself and am more knowledgeable about stroke.

Returning home provided the jump start I needed to keep my recovery moving forward. Suddenly there was a smorgasbord of activities with eternal value which required me to get better in order to enjoy full participation. Now that's some good incentive for improvement.

Since I'm the only one in our home who understands personally how challenging and frustrating it is to journey through life with a brain injury, I look for opportunities to meet other stroke survivors. Most of these connections are made through my volunteer work with the American Stroke Association, a division of the American Heart Association.

It's obvious Troy sometimes gets frustrated with how my new mind works. One evening recently, I wasn't up for any input on something I'd done which wasn't quite right and as a preemptive strike said, "Look. If you get annoyed with where my thinking sometimes leads me, you should be grateful you don't depend on my brain 24/7." That comment seemed to help him keep the current annoyance in perspective.

Thank God Jesus Christ's sacrifice provides a way for us to make a new start in life, when we're ready. I like how the Winter Warlock puts it in the Christmas movie mentioned earlier. He sings, "If I want to change the reflection I see in the mirror each morn, you mean that it's just my election, to vote for a chance to be **reborn**?" The words *reborn* and *born again* have been bastardized in modern society, but they originally described the truism that each person has until death to reconnect with God by accepting Jesus Christ as her personal Lord and Savior. God tells us in 2 Corinthians 5:17 that, "Therefore if any man be in Christ, he is a new creature: old things are passed away; behold, all things are become new."

Accepting Jesus' sacrifice is the most significant turning point in a person's life because she's separated from God by sin until being saved. Information about taking that leap of faith is included in the *Epilogue*. Most folks don't know when their life will end, but we do know each life ends someday. God created humans as mortal beings, so each of us will no longer need our body, one day. When that day comes, our soul will relocate either to Heaven or hell for all of eternity.

Heaven and hell aren't physically described in the Bible but the level of comfort or discomfort a soul will experience in each location is clear. Do I want to spend eternity reunited with God or separated from Him? Once I understood the situation that way, relinquishing control over my life and asking for forgiveness was an easy choice to make.

Control is another stumbling block toward salvation. It took me about six years post-stroke to assign meaning to the saying, "Let go and let God." I've come to believe God has His plan and nothing we do will change it. He doesn't waste His time micro-managing what each of us does because that would undermine Him having created us with free will. God's Holy Spirit does, however, provide guidance to any saved person who asks, "What's next, Lord?"

To become a new creature in Christ is as simple as acknowledging Jesus Christ died and was resurrected for the forgiveness of our sins. Pride seems to be the stumbling block for many people, who think they can earn a spot in Heaven through good works on Earth. That's not how it works. Admission to Heaven is free and easy, requiring only that a person acknowledge she can't control her own admission, except by relinquishing that control.

Princess Margaret, younger sister of Queen Elizabeth II, died of stroke at 71.

CHAPTER 9

FLOATIN' MY OWN BOAT AGAIN

> **SideNote:** Notes about the six years I returned to work surfaced periodically as I wrote previous chapters. These thoughts didn't seem to fit anywhere but I kept them in a separate file in case I needed them later. Then, while writing *There's No Place Like Home*, I began to view my return to work as a cornerstone in my recovery.

It had been easy to bury memories about my return to work because it was so challenging and frustrating. There's nothing like an apples-to-apples comparison to identify what's different about a person. Only after deliberately looking for ways God had guided me through that time did I see the headway I'd made both spiritually and cognitively. The work opportunities which fueled these gains wouldn't have presented themselves had I remained on disability.

I never seriously considered staying on disability for too long because that would have been contrary to

Gee, I wish... ...I'd taken an Arctic cruise.

my *go-get-'em* personality. Rather, I focused on convincing others I should get back to work as soon as possible. My hasty return to work wasn't all my idea; Troy seemed to think it'd be good for me to get back in my old groove, too. The colleagues who took turns delivering meals to our home fueled my fire with comments like, "You seem like the same E to me," "I think you're ready to get back to work," and "We sure could use your help."

Only my rehab doctor, Dr. Denny, expressed reservations about my quick return to work. After several conversations, he relented and approved me to begin working up to three hours a day, up to three days a week, effective June 26. Apparently I'd convinced him I understood the pros and cons of returning to work. In reality, I had no idea what I was getting myself into. What can I say? My mouth continued to work quite well, in most situations, despite there being little or no thought behind my words.

Talk about throwing fuel on a fire. Two weeks at home wasn't Even an unborn baby can suffer a stroke.
nearly long enough for me to relearn what's expected of me as a wife and mom. Trying to get things back to *normal* at home wasn't working too well for me when suddenly, I found myself facing similar challenges at work. What I hadn't yet figured out is that a person's life **doesn't** return to *normal* after stroke. With a great deal of faith and effort, things can get back on an even keel, however. When a survivor reaches this milestone, he's well on his way toward developing his new definition of *normal*.

Although I'd like to say my return to work went more smoothly than my move back home, this **is** a non-fiction work. The company had been progressing quite well since being founded some 80 years earlier, and that progress hadn't been impacted by my time away. Others had stepped up to provide the communications materials I'd previously authored. The fact the business had survived without me kind of hurt.

I have scant memories of my first day back other than feeling really awkward. It was weird enough I had to ride to work with Troy because I didn't yet have my driver's license back. Then, my manager met me at the front door to show me to my office, alleg-edly because our area had been rearranged in my absence. Do you suppose he did that to ensure I didn't get lost trying to find my own desk? People began filtering through the doorway to welcome me back as I gazed at the moving boxes in my office.

These were folks I'd had a solid, professional relationship with pre-stroke. It was then I began to grasp how the damage to the vi-sual areas of my brain affects my life. None of their bright, smiling faces looked remotely familiar. It was if I'd never seen them before. Then, as each one spoke, I found I could retrieve their name based on their voice.

The look of shock on most of those faces was so obvious even I noticed it. This wasn't a simple look of surprise but rather an expres-sion that said, "Wow! She did live, and she looks just like she did the last time I saw her." After the obligatory, "Hi. Welcome back. How are the boys?" kind of comments, most of my colleagues ran out of things to say.

These folks surely remembered me as a dedicated, well-respect-ed employee who always had a good comeback on the tip of her tongue. They had no idea what to make of my re-appearance, how-ever, or what to say to me. This was an early clue my return to work would be a beneficial, albeit painful, learning experience for all involved.

When Mick, whom I consider a friend and colleague, stopped by, I asked him why everyone seemed so shocked to see me. He generally has a good one-liner handy and this time said, "Well you know, E, it's not like you had an appendectomy or something! Most folks probably didn't expect to ever see you again and don't know what to say to you." In lieu of knowing what to say, several people said, "God wasn't ready for you yet."

That statement so confounded me I finally asked our pastor what it means. He politely explained it's a platitude and has no real meaning. The best line I heard was, "E, you know, if you needed some attention, all you had to do was ask for it!" Good advice… from another communications professional.

It was only natural folks didn't know what to say to me; I didn't

know how to handle the situation either. It's not like most people
have experience interacting with a high-functioning brain injury
survivor. Some folks might have seen a person fade away from Alzheimer's disease, which spares the body while killing the brain. I
imagine people react in a similar way as the progressive brain damage of that disease changes a loved one's *cognitive blueprint*. One key
difference between Alzheimer's and stroke, however, is that stroke
suddenly changes the brain; there's nothing gradual about it.

My colleagues may have also been wondering what to expect of
me. Fair enough…considering I didn't even know what to expect
of myself. Besides, I'm sure they knew I'd only been cleared to
work nine hours a week. How much can a person accomplish in
that amount of time? For crying-out-loud, I sleep more than that
each day.

Although I didn't recognize what was different about my thinking ability, most of my colleagues quickly realized I couldn't con-
tribute to the business's success as I had in the past. If they needed
help with a challenging project, they learned to bypass me and ask
my manager for assistance. Being a kind-hearted soul, he'd either
do the work himself or assign it to someone else. Not the best solution, perhaps, but it provided a way to avoid the underlying issue:
I could no longer function at the level required by my job, and no
one seemed willing to broach that topic with me.

In an attempt to bolster my crushed self-confidence, my manager even found some projects for me to complete that were so
well-defined I could succeed at them by following steps defined
by someone else. This rote approach to communicating wasn't my
style, but at least I was contributing something at work.

Others were involved in this facade, too. A couple of folks really went out of their way to help rebuild my confidence. They'd
put together their own communication plan, write the materials,
and ask me to edit their work. Since they were the subject-matter
experts, I figured that was an okay process. Besides, my ability to
edit seemed unscathed, as I pointed out errors in grammar and
style. That sure seems like a lot of effort, by a lot of people, to avoid
calling a spade a spade.

These early attempts to help me succeed remind me that if you must choose between being kind or honest in a relationship, it's better to go with the honest option. You may not feel too kind when you tell someone the cold, hard truth, but it's hurtful to pretend things are alright when they aren't really going so well.

It'd be great if everyone would be honest **and** kind at all times, but that's not how things work. Telling a brain injury survivor the facts in a kind way has to be doubly challenging because he may not grasp the meaning behind your words no matter how, or how often, you say them. For anyone struggling to come to terms with a life permanently altered by brain injury, getting honest feedback from trusted others is absolutely critical, though.

Trust me; any stroke survivor you happen to know is probably struggling to figure out what happened and, more importantly, what's next. He certainly doesn't need to hear a bunch of feel-good mumbo-jumbo from others. Be kind to him but, more importantly, be honest. You may have learned as a child that if you can't think of something nice to say, don't say anything at all. As an alternative, try making three kind comments for each bit of (potentially) hurtful, honest feedback you share.

Several colleagues probably tried to help me understand I wasn't functioning too well, but I didn't *hear* them. Okay, technically, I heard them. I may even have agreed with some of their comments. That didn't mean I had a clue what I should do with the information they shared. For others to notice what's different about me before I'd noticed it myself was unnerving. Surely I'd notice if something was wrong with my own mind, wouldn't I? Based on personal experience, I now know that's not (necessarily) how it works. This reality helped me realize the benefits of accepting unsolicited feedback without comment, *thinking on* what I heard, and then seeking additional input.

At one point, things got so awkward at work I asked Dr. Lee, the neuropsychologist I'd worked with at the Center, to come to a staff meeting and give my colleagues tips on how to interact with me. Surely our failure to communicate was their responsibility, not mine. They just needed more information about my situation.

Dr. Lee did a fine job of summarizing what my colleagues could reasonably expect of me and how they could help me succeed. However, I think his comments simply left them wondering how long I'd be left languishing before someone decided I should go recover somewhere else. The thought was certainly on my mind.

Dr. Denny gradually increased the number of hours I was allowed to work during my first three months back to work. Naturally, I worked the maximum allowable hours each week because I was intent on getting back into the swing of things. My restricted work hours had me so annoyed I overlooked the fact I was too tired to fill my at-home roles of wife and mom.

The responsibilities and (perceived) control I'd had at work before my stroke looked so appealing. When I approached Dr. Denny about being released from disability and returning to work full time, he expressed his concerns much more directly than before. As I recall, he likened my release from disability to jumping off a cliff. It was a big step, and there was no way to undo the deed once it was done. Was I sure I was ready to dive back into the big world of business? I convinced Dr. Denny the time had come and he signed the paperwork, effective Oct. 2, 2000. Ha! With his work restriction out of the way, I was confident I'd regain my spot at work.

I didn't make much headway toward that goal in the ensuing six years. Instead, I was sort of bounced around among managers and assigned a variety of well-defined responsibilities. No one seemed to have the time or energy to confront the underlying issue of my changed abilities, but no one wanted to push me out the door, either.

Then I found myself reporting to Tricia, an observant, honest individual who really helped me get my bearings. With her help, I came to realize my mind lacked the laser-sharp focus I'd relied on in the past. She helped me realize my ability to process what I heard went out the window if I was bored, overwhelmed by the magnitude of a topic, opposed to what I heard, or thinking of how I'd have presented the information.

Rather than whacking me upside the head with these observations, Tricia shared them with me honestly and kindly. Then, after earning my respect and trust, she toppled a domino in the picture of my post-stroke life by pointing out, "Your heart's no longer in your job, E." Simple, honest statements often pack an incredible punch, and this was no exception. She'd figured out the personal connection I'd once felt with my work was gone. I'd been just going through the motions since my return to work. The tasks I'd completed in that time justified the compensation I received and the progress I'd made in my recovery justified the time I'd spent, but my job no longer helped me feel whole.

Tricia's comment helped me realize Corporate America was no longer the best place to use my communication skills. I've only worked professionally within one company, and happen to think any other business would be a step-down. That thought process led me to make a connection, a rare post-stroke occurrence for me. I figured-out there's nothing here on Earth which could ever make me feel fulfilled, long-term. Reaching that conclusion really took the wind out of my sails. Coming to terms with the fact I'm mortal — and had very nearly proven it — had somehow caused the old emptiness mentioned earlier to well up again.

As I see it, when God breathed the breath of life into Adam's nostrils (Genesis 2:7), He ensured all human beings would sense His existence, at some level. Each person seems to have a lingering feeling there must be Someone of divine significance in-charge. This *hunch* caused an aching emptiness in me from the time I was a young child until the day I was saved. No matter what I accomplished or experienced in the meantime, that emptiness was ever-present.

Another way I think of the breath of God is to picture it as a spark of the Divine.

Getting reconnected with God through the Grace provided by Jesus Christ was the only way I'd ever feel whole. Some people readily accept Jesus' sacrifice as soon as they learn about it; others flat-out refuse to accept He died for us. A third type of person, including me, accepts His gift only after much time and reflection.

I'd been struggling with that issue for several months by then and had felt God's influence on my thoughts. That void had grown bigger and stronger than before and seemed to be pulling at my heart and mind with the power of a black hole. My job had provided a way to fill that void, at least temporarily, pre-stroke. Now I knew there was nothing I could do to control it; I could no longer even hope to contain it.

The fact I had a check-up scheduled with my primary care physician later that day strikes me as a convergence of cues the Holy Spirit had provided different people. Some may say it was coincidence or luck, but I'm not buying it. Tricia stopped me on my way out of the office and made me promise to call her when I got home from my appointment. She was worried about my state of mind, and rightfully so.

When I arrived at Dr. Don's that afternoon, his usual question, "How's everything going for you at work, at home, and out in the world, E?" prompted an unusual response. I started to cry. Okay, I crashed and burned as we talked. Bottom line, it was the biggest flood since Noah's day. Dr. Don had seen one of his med school roommates plunge into depression after her stroke and was quick to recognize I, too, was in the throws of depression.

By the end of my appointment, I'd agreed to begin taking an anti-depressant and to go back on disability. This was a powerful moment of self awareness. Acknowledging I *might* need that medicine initially prompted me to feel like a wimp because I'd always been a very positive, can-do kind of person. As I drove home from my check-up, the Holy Spirit was nudging me to leave the rat race and tell the world what Jesus Christ has done, is doing, and will do for me.

This was the day the emptiness I'd sensed in my soul since I was a young child became overwhelming. I bottomed out. I'd been like a vacuum for years… *glomming* onto almost anything that seemed like a good fit but still having room for more-and-more. As I realized my stroke had limited my ability to fill that emptiness with material things, I began to sense the only way I'd ever feel truly whole.

After filling my prescription, I went home, crawled into bed, and called Troy to tell him I was going back on disability. Hmmm…

I hadn't planned to mention that until Troy got home from work. After confiding in him, I felt oddly calm. He took the news in-stride and asked what I planned to do next. Both of us seemed surprised when I said, "I'm not sure what's next, but I know God has something planned for me. Besides, you know I believe things always work-out." Troy keeps track of all financial particulars in our home and may have felt a panicky sensation sneaking up on him. If so, he kept it to himself and ended our brief call with some assurance everything would be okay.

Funny thing… I'd planned to tell Troy about my return to dis-ability when he got home that day and yet I'd spilled the beans, accurately and concisely during our call.

Another fork appeared in my road when I handed my life over to Christ. As I sat on our bed sobbing, only God and our cats were listening. I poured out all of the frustrations and fears I'd been harboring. How I'd been hoping no one would notice I wasn't the same person I'd been pre-stroke.

They heard me say I wasn't even interested in what seemed so important to everyone else. No measure of worldly success made any difference to me. I told them I love my God and my family, and the more I recovered, the further I felt from them.

Then I called my manager to assure her I was okay. I also told Tricia I wouldn't be into work the next day because my doctor said I should be on disability leave. She helped me get that process start-ed, made me promise to take care of myself, and hung-up. Oddly enough, I hadn't planned to mention disability when I called Tri-cia, yet I'd rattled-off that part of our conversation without a hitch, or a tear.

My next step was calling my friend, Bea, to let her know what Dr. Don had said. She wasn't surprised by his diagnosis and was relieved to hear he'd prescribed an anti-depressant. Next thing I knew, I heard myself asking Bea to meet me at my place of employ-ment at 5 o'clock the next morning. We exercise at the local YMCA early each day, but she was fine with varying our work-out that day. Somehow I knew Bea could help me remain calm as I gathered the 18+ years of sundry stuff I had in my office. All of it belonged to me, and I didn't want it to be pitched in my *absence*.

How bizarre… I hadn't planned to ask Bea for moving assistance when I called yet I'd made arrangements to pack-up my professional life before we hung-up.

Then I did what any reasonable person should do: I turned my burden over to God. Prayer is a private conversation with God, in my opinion.

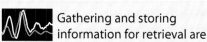

Gathering and storing information for retrieval are **basic** brain activities. The ability to make connections among disparate bits of information and reach a logical conclusion is more advanced.

What I tell and ask God is strictly my business, as is how and what I hear back from Him. That's why I generally keep my prayers to myself. However, you need to know what I cried out to God that afternoon because it triggered a key step forward in my life.

God's love for me is so great He waited almost 40 years for me to recognize that His Son, Jesus Christ, had died in atonement for my sins. Simply sensing God's existence and wanting to know Him kept me alive, until then. You see, God established a link with Adam by breathing life into his nostrils. That link still exists between God and each person.

Better yet, you can get reconnected with God simply by accepting that Jesus Christ died so your sins would be forgiven, too. Recovering from a massive stroke provided the time and space I needed to accept Christ's selfless gift.

With more emotion than I knew I had, I thanked God for opening the doors of Heaven to me by sending His only Son to die in my place, so my sins could be forgiven. Next, I apologized for taking almost 40 years to figure out what Jesus' sacrifice means to me. Then, I gratefully accepted that sacrifice and asked God to walk through the rest of this life with me. In conclusion, I popped the big question, "What's next, Lord?" I'd gotten over any, "Why me, God?" qualms quite some time before.

This was the day I finally heard God tell me I was on the wrong boat. Although He'd been hinting I should get out of my boat and follow Him, I didn't actually hear Him until I wiped the stain of sin from my life. I knew then and there it was time to get my feet wet, like Peter does in Matthew 14:27-33. It took six and a half years for me to reach the point where I could let go and take that walk. When I got out of my old boat, I realized the water was just fine.

The Holy Spirit conveyed this message by helping me realize the thoughts ricocheting around in my mind had assembled themselves in a coherent sequence. Said another way, God nudged me to listen to the logical conclusion my brain had reached. This gentle approach to guidance makes sense given that God knows every thought that passes through our mind, but lets us think things out according to our own free will.

Simply put, my mind had done what the late, great Yogi Berra advised years earlier, "When you come to a fork in the road, take it!" If you're thinking that's the only option, think again. I could have simply stopped moving forward. This option, AKA quitting, isn't open to me, however, because I know God has a plan for me. I don't know exactly what His plan is, obviously. That's for God to know and me to find out… when I'm reunited with Him in Heaven.

For the first time in my life, I heard His answer clearly. In no uncertain terms, the Holy Spirit led me to start using my communication skills to glorify God. My triumphant, post-stroke return to work ended that day as my focus shifted from reclaiming my place in the world to things above (Colossians 3:2). Corporate America would have to forge ahead without me.

Immediately, I was overwhelmed by a feeling of tranquility and purpose unlike any I'd experienced before. Then, a clear, bright idea entered my mind. I should start investing my communication skills to bring glory to God. Specifically, I should write a book about how God got my attention by capitalizing on how stroke had changed my life.

As confirmation I'd identified my purpose in life, the enemy began attacking my idea almost instantly with questions such as, "How can you possibly want to glorify God after what you've been through?" and "How you gonna explain **this one** to Troy?" It was too late for him to change my mind, though. My sights had already refocused on things above.

After defeating that attack of *maybe-this-isn't-such-a-good-idea*, I decided my book would focus on helping others understand that God doesn't let bad things happen to good people. Rather, He waits patiently for each of us to accept Jesus Christ as our personal Lord and Savior so His Holy Spirit can lead us through this world before He welcomes us into Heaven, when the time comes. My Sunday School teachers had taught me that back in the 1970s, but I didn't really think I needed God back then.

The beauty of this life is that God has a plan for each of us. He created us with free will and has been letting us do our own thing from the get-go. Those of us following the Holy Spirit's cues are on the path to fulfilling God's plan for us. He doesn't force us to do or become anything in particular but as a longtime friend of mine says, "God does a lot of hinting." After cleansing your soul of sin, all you need to do is watch and listen. His hints will become apparent to you.

Also, God never leads a person to do something inconsistent with His Word. God has the power to shut-down this world, and will when He decides the time has come, but He's anything but a micromanager. That means God isn't the cause of the hurricanes, world hunger, wars, accidents, diseases, and other terrors in our world. We've brought such tragedies on ourselves by being irresponsible with our free will. Although God surely suffers when He sees the pain we bring ourselves, why would He deny us of our free will by preventing natural consequences?

Ariel Sharon, prime minister of Israel, died of stroke at 80.

CHAPTER 10

IN SIGHT, OUT OF MIND

To me, the most noticeable impact of my stroke is on how my brain handles visual information. Having gotten my first pair of glasses in 3rd grade, I'm no stranger to vision challenges. Back then, near-sightedness was my only vision problem as I struggled to read the chalkboard. However, with the vision areas of my brain *rearranged* by stroke, I now have an interesting assortment of challenges. My visual acuity can't be blamed for these because I still have 20/20 vision, with glasses.

With one tweak, the old saying, "out of sight, out of mind" works well to describe my post-stroke vision challenges. I'm now surrounded by things that are **in** sight, but **out** of mind. This change is the result of stroke killing countless brain cells and snapping several neurological connections.

I hadn't seen *photo-greys* in years, and when I asked the wearer who made them, she had no idea what I was talking about. Turns out those are called progressive lenses, these days.

Gee,
I wish...
...I'd appreciated
my vision more.

This chapter describes some of my more *interesting* visual challenges. Let me assure you if you looked <u>at my eyes</u>, you wouldn't see any evidence of these challenges. However, if you could see <u>through my eyes</u>, you'd notice what's different about my view.

My brain's diminished ability to communicate with my left eye causes certain vision challenges. Said another way, I <u>can</u> see with my left eye, it's just that I often <u>don't</u> see with it, unless I remind myself to *look left*. To see what's happening to my left, I must constantly remind myself half of the world is over there and prep myself for what I may see.

As a result of this deficit, I didn't drive for about 18 months poststroke. My license had expired the day after I entered the hospital, coincidentally, and it took that long for me to feel confident I could drive safely, once again.

When my brain tells my eyes to look down, my right eye 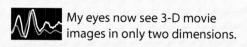 My eyes now see 3-D movie images in only two dimensions. hears, "Look down," and automatically rotates downward. In contrast, the left eye hears something akin to, "Ook-lay own-day," and has to translate the message. Both eyes get the same message from my brain, but there's a delay while the left eye translates instructions. By the time my left eye deciphers the message and responds, the right eye has a head start and the two are out-of-sync.

Of course, since I'm determined to keep getting better for the rest of my life, I occasionally force both eyes to look straight ahead. This hasn't been a positive experience, to date. I feel an odd pull behind my left eye and see a whirling pattern rather than distinct objects.

When my eyes do zero-in on something, it's a struggle for them to work with the right half of my brain to *accurately* assign meaning to it. As a result, I see the world differently than I did for 33 years, and often see it in a way those around me find unusual.

Occasionally, one of our boys will try to spell something in the air with his finger. This approach to communicating doesn't work for me, even on a good day. Trying to follow his finger is challenging enough, let alone trying to visualize what letter he's crafting.

Our visual-spatial abilities depend on seamless, two-way communication between our eyes and brain. The brain tells our muscles where to direct our eyes, receives information from the eyes, processes that information, and tells our eyes what to do next. It may also tell other body parts how to respond based on information received visually.

When we see something, information gathered by our eyes automatically flows into our brain to be integrated with other information. What we see may prompt us to:

- Move some body part(s);
- File the information away for future use; or
- Ignore it.

Like most folks, I could see and make sense of what I saw from a young age. My pre-stroke educational and professional experiences provided ample opportunities to hone my *adequate* visual spatial abilities into a unique skill which often distinguished me from my peers. Over time, I learned to **automatically** see the big picture. I'd notice what was going on, understand new information, see how that information fit into the big picture, identify underlying details that would be affected, and respond accordingly.

Most of those around me didn't seem to have that ability so I often found myself, prior to my stroke, explaining how I'd reached a conclusion that was crystal-clear only to me. This ability was so natural I didn't take time to consider how it **really** worked.

These days I have to really concentrate to see the big picture in the right side of my brain. After the big picture fades in, I must intentionally redirect my attention toward obtaining related details from the left side of my brain.

It took more than six years for me to emerge from this denial and accept the fact my brain now speaks a different language than my left eye. It's as if it still speaks English to my right eye but uses Pig Latin with the left. If all goes well, I get the details I need to create the big picture I envisioned.

If you're wondering why it took so long for me to figure out I no longer see things the way I used to, consider this. How can a person figure out she sees the world differently than others when she does, in fact, see the world differently than most people? As a simple example, if I'm sure the shoes I'm wearing are black and my husband says black shoes would look better with that outfit, whose eyes are off?

Identifying this challenge strikes me as a classic Catch22. That may help explain why it took so long for me to identify this cognitive deficit and others which have since surfaced. Besides, my brain was focused on regaining control over each paralyzed body part before it could shift into fixing how it handles visual information.

After accepting the fact my visual spatial abilities had changed, I began learning about our ability to see. We humans need both innate and learned skills to see, derive meaning from what we see, and respond appropriately. Any or all steps required to see and understand can be affected by injury to the vision areas of the brain. Since much of the information absorbed by humans is collected visually, changes in my visual spatial abilities have a big impact on my life.

The more I learned, it began to dawn on me that I'm now often oblivious to what those around me automatically see and understand. My new understanding led me to empathize with Hans Christian Anderson's naked emperor. For him to realize he wasn't wearing any clothes strikes me as very similar to the shock I felt when I realized I'm often no longer *in-the-know*. Okay, so it took a while for me to connect the dots; the emperor probably felt a little slow, too.

Many of those close to me recognized problems with my vision long before I did, and had been trying to help me understand what was different. I knew the tables had been turned when that realization dawned on me. Others had seen something before me and I was the one who was slow-on-the-uptake. Worse yet, the conclusion they'd reached was about me. I'm so grateful I wasn't in their shoes, stuck trying to help me understand my visual losses.

I still cringe when I vaguely recall Troy telling me it was inappropriate for me to wear yellow sweatpants to work one *casual* Friday. Something about the unusual color of those pants told me they'd blend-in just fine with what my colleagues would be wearing. Troy did his best to convince me I was under-dressed, but I informed him everyone would be dressed casually. Besides, it wasn't like I was wearing common, grey sweatpants, and the T-shirt I wore matched them perfectly. Troy knew better than to push the topic too far and simply rolled his eyes.

He was right, of course. Those clothes were inappropriate for my job any day of the week. I wouldn't even have worn them to work on one of the marathon weekend days I'd put in prior to my stroke. Although no one at work said anything to me about attire that day, I imagine there were some offline comments akin to, "Oh, that's just E—at least she's still with us…"

As with other deficits mentioned earlier, my vision challenges are different than those I've seen other stroke survivors battle. I've met survivors who no longer recognize familiar faces, objects, letters, or numbers. I even met a woman whose stroke made it impossible for her to deliberately move either eye. As a result, her eyes rolled wherever they chose, independent of one another. I feel fortunate to have only my set of challenges to overcome.

Each stroke survivor has a unique set of deficits, which vary depending on the severity and location of her brain injury.

When I shift my gaze toward a near object after looking at something far away or vice versa there's a noticeable delay as the *new* object comes into focus. I really notice this problem at sporting events where it's no longer worth the effort to watch both the scoreboard and the game. I just go with one or the other.

The delay is a communication, rather than muscle, problem. My left eye and the muscles which move it are just fine. It's the garbled communication between the right hemisphere of my brain and left eye that causes problems. I'm told this loss first presented itself during in-patient therapy a few weeks after my stroke when a physical therapist noticed I was struggling to relearn to walk. Tammy suspected my vision was out-of-whack and requested an eye exam, which confirmed my stroke had shifted my visual midline. This means that when I look straight ahead, the world appears to be at an angle.

If you've ever walked across a tilted floor in an amusement park fun house, you've experienced a temporary shift in your visual midline. Relearning to walk is tough enough when you've been laying flat on your back for weeks and have only recently learned you have a left half. The added complexity of seeing the floor at an angle while negotiating your next step is a bit much. Yoked prism glasses were prescribed to level-out my environment during therapy. These funky, nerd glasses tricked me into seeing the floor as level, which of course it was. With the gym floor evened out, I continued making progress in PT.

Although I graduated from the nerd glasses pretty quickly, my visual midline is still a bit off-center. I've adapted to this reality by keeping my head cocked to the left and assuming a posture some might describe as odd. Basically, I lean back, forward, or to the side when standing or sitting. As a result, my balance isn't so good, I'm a bit clumsy, and I move somewhat robotically. I also seem to gravitate toward the right side of rooms and hallways, perhaps because it's difficult for me to keep track of where *straight-ahead* is.

Something about this challenge makes it very disorienting to have both feet off the ground at the same time, which makes running a very frightening thing, indeed. I've never really **liked** to run but it would be nice to be able to dash inside from my car when it's raining. This loss also makes it tough to fish an object out of a container, which is most noticeable when I want to get something out of my car console while driving. Since I need to look directly at the object I'm trying to retrieve, I opt to pull-over and find it.

If this challenge sounds like a simple, little glitch to you, consider this. Our eyes are designed to work together so our brain can gauge distance and depth. By working together, our eyes also help us keep track of where we are relative to our surroundings. These visual-cognitive abilities help us stay oriented, maintain our balance, and move smoothly. They also require having both eyes focused on the same object at the same time.

Since my brain and left eye now speak different languages, my depth perception is inaccurate. In addition to some accommodations mentioned later, I manage this challenge by deliberately reminding myself to pay attention to how things are situated, relative to one another. Tiring, yet effective.

Most likely, you automatically get a sense of how much room is between things as you look at them. I, however, have to remind myself to note how they're positioned. This makes driving a bit of an adventure but I've found some ways to keep it as safe as possible.

Of course, my tilted view becomes more skewed when I'm fatigued or ill. When that happens, my balance is really bad, and I have trouble using my vision to guide my left arm, hand, leg, and foot. This loss seldom affects my daily life now but once, while walking near our home, I suddenly felt like I was falling over. When I looked down to see what was going on, I noticed the sidewalk I was on had a very definite tilt. I'd walked that path hundreds of times, both pre- and post-stroke, and had never noticed the incline. My balance must have been *off* just enough that day to make the incline a concern. Naturally, I first questioned the location of my feet rather than the sidewalk.

I mentioned my most bothersome visual challenge, left neglect, earlier. Like many brain injury survivors, I tend to overlook what's happening on my affected side, the side opposite my injury. Since my right hemisphere has an injury, I have left neglect. Although my five senses should automatically keep me aware of what's going on over there, they don't.

This loss limits the effectiveness of all five senses but my vision is the most noticeably impacted. If an object isn't in my direct line-of-sight, I don't automatically see it, especially if it's off to my left. For example, Troy and I took our sons to get haircuts a week or so after I moved back home. When the boys were done, Troy asked the stylist to, "Level her off, too." When I asked what in the world he meant by that, Troy said the hair on the left side of my head was much longer than that on the right. Since I'd never heard of stroke causing hair to grow faster on one side of a person's head than the other, I asked Troy what he meant.

He explained that my head had been shaved prior to surgery on March 7. Troy then told me only the right side was shaved in preparation for my follow-up surgery on March 30. Of course my hair was longer on the left side; it had a 3-week head start. When I reached up to see if the left side really was longer, I was shocked. I'd been washing, brushing, and styling my own hair for several weeks and had never noticed the difference in length. Left neglect was at work. And, my hair did look much better after it was *leveled off.*

My left neglect often leads to humorous situations, such as when Trent asked, while riding in the car with me, how I'd gotten sunburned. He was sitting in the back seat and could see only the left half of my face. Since I knew I wasn't sunburned, I glanced in the mirror to see what prompted his question. Naturally, I noticed the right side of my face first, and it looked fine. However, when I looked at my left side, it did, in fact, look sunburned. That's when I realized I'd only put make-up on the right side of my face. Whoops. I had some touch-up work to do when we reached our destination.

Don's encounter with my neglect problem was a bit more humorous. While using my legs as a backrest, he ran a hand up and down each shin. "Mom, how come only one of your legs has hair?" Don asked. After reaching down to feel what prompted his question, I said, "You know, Don, they both have hair, it's just that I forgot about leftie the last time I shaved."

One of my more frightening neglect moments occurred on the interstate. As I began merging to my left, I very nearly missed *parking* my car under a semi. I've no idea how long that huge chunk of metal had been there but it obviously hadn't just appeared. It had snuck-up on my *blind* side. This episode brought back fond memories of Dad saying, "Always look before you change lanes. Never trust your mirrors!" Telling me to turn my head and look was good advice the first time I learned to drive and it still works. Back then I sometimes didn't notice driving hazards because I was 16.

Although it can be tough to get my attention for other reasons these days, physically turning my head does help me see better. Things don't just *catch my eye* but if I go to the trouble of moving my head, it's kind of like there ought to be something to see. When I check the lane beside me, I'm looking for visual proof there's an opening, not a vehicle I should avoid. Somehow, I appreciate knowing there's an opening more than resenting there isn't room to merge, kind of like I see a glass as half-full rather than half-empty.

> **SideNote**: Speaking of that old dichotomy, I realized recently it would be fine to say a glass is at half-capacity.

The left side of my body sometimes *merges* into objects when I'm walking, too. These collisions often result in bruises on my left arm or leg. Since the left side of my body is less sensitive to pain than my right, I seldom notice these marks until someone asks me what happened. I've had some pretty impressive bruises on my left side with no idea how I got them.

Aside from not seeing some things that do exist, I also now see some things that aren't real. It's more fun to think of these as *hallucinations*, so I'll go with that term.

One hallucination I've come to *appreciate* is what I call Grey Bar Syndrome. If I let myself get overly tired or am getting ill, I first feel a bit dizzy and nauseous. If I don't respond to those warning signs by taking a nap, a swirling pattern appears in my left eye and I notice a **significant** delay in communication between that eye and my brain. If I still choose to forge ahead rather than listening to my body, a vertical, grey bar appears in my left eye. Although I can see around this hallucination, it distorts what I see and makes me feel more nauseous. Seeing the world through a grey bar over my left eye is a bit like looking through a glop of *sleep* in my eye. However, this bar is much more distinct and no amount of wiping or rubbing removes it. The only way I've found to get rid of the grey bar is a good nap.

If the boys want to go somewhere when I sense the grey bar appearing, all I need to say is, "Not right now, I have a grey bar." They understand what that means and seem to appreciate the fact I'm unwilling to drive when my vision's messed up. This grey bar is an hallucination, one of the many visual deficits common to brain injury survivors.

My other stroke-induced hallucinations involve a tendency for stationary objects (poles, steps, and the like) to occasionally look like they're in-motion. Pretty dull hallucinations, eh? As with other deficits, fatigue and illness intensify my tendency to hallucinate.

Predictably, my visual abilities are further diminished in distracting situations. The most challenging ones are those which are emotionally loaded, move at an unpredictable pace, have too many visuals to attend to, or are loaded with new information.

To limit these distractions, I try to look only for a specific object, and only after describing it to myself. For example, if there's a big pile of stuff in our family room, I won't automatically see any of the objects in that pile. However, if I tell myself I'm looking for one specific object and describe it to myself; I may see it in the pile. I suppose that's a good reason to break my packratting habit, huh?

A related challenge is my limited ability to see things placed where they don't belong. For example, I once sat on our cat, Pawz, after laying a pillow and blanket next to her on the couch. I didn't see her there because my mind didn't expect her to be there. Couches are for people, right? She *shouldn't* have been there, so my mind told me she wasn't.

Another reason I sometimes don't see what others do is that visualization is no longer automatic for me. Our ability to visualize helps us assign order to our surroundings and makes our life more colorful. Chances are you've already used your ability to visualize objects several times today. Perhaps you made a mental note of where you parked your car or where you left the TV remote?

Maybe you visualized how different pieces of the outfit you're wearing would look together before getting dressed? Maybe you can quickly find things on your desk because you keep a mental map of where you set things? Hopefully, you remember where you parked your bike or car, too.

It took about three years post-stroke for me to realize I no longer *pictured* anything in my mind. A cognitive therapist helped me pinpoint this loss by having me review a picture and then (try to) tell her what I'd seen. It was a bit unnerving to stare intently at a picture for several seconds, close my eyes, try to visualize what I'd just seen, and see only black.

That's what happened the first few times Brandy and I started working through this exercise. As I got more and more concerned about my inability to visualize things, she'd start dropping hints about what was in the picture I'd seen. As she spoke, I found I could connect her words with what I'd seen and an image of the picture would slowly appear in my mind.

BrainBuzz was a familiar gremlin by that point in my recovery but the cognitive energy generated by this exercise set-off a 4-alarm clanging inside my skull. I was genuinely afraid I'd be unable to drive home safely from that therapy session.

My dad used to tell me I was the only person he'd ever known who could get lost in her own backyard. To his credit, Dad hasn't said that since my stroke. Perhaps he knows I'm prone to getting disoriented and lost wherever I go. Since regaining my ability to visualize, life has gradually gotten easier. My fear of getting lost diminished as I got comfortable being able to picture where I'd parked or where I'd seen a certain section in a store.

A comparison may help you relate to what it's like to view the world with stroke-impaired vision. If you've ever watched a movie while reading its subtitles, you may have noticed it's tough to enjoy the images because your attention is divided between the picture and the words. The images are as good as ever but your appreciation and understanding of what's shown is diminished because your attention is divided between seeing the picture and reading the words. The visual challenges created by my stroke require my brain to divide its attention between telling itself what to do and communicating with my eyes.

Having opened this chapter with "out of sight, out of mind," I'll close by saying my stroke brought God, Who is out of sight, into my mind and heart. I began seeing the world through my new set of God lenses on Jan. 30, 2000, and will enjoy that view for the rest of my days. Perhaps I can see and appreciate His majesty now because I deal with only half of the world automatically. If my eyes and brain were on full speaking terms, I believe I'd still be oblivious to His Glory.

Is it really any wonder the human brain is such a splendid design? "…God created man in his own image… male and female created he them," says Genesis 1:27. So that's why each individual part of our body is an engineering marvel. That also explains the amazing teamwork our body displays when those parts work together as designed.

Mae West, a popular American actress, died of stroke at 87.

CHAPTER 11

GOTTA HAVE
A GAME PLAN

Your brain works 24/7 simply keeping you alive. It regulates your heartbeat, breathing, body temperature, and a variety of other life-sustaining functions. In addition, it automatically interprets information absorbed by your five senses (feel, see, hear, taste, and smell) and tells your body how to respond. If your brain gets injured, it may become unable to meet your basic survival needs, let alone communicate with specific body parts.

My brain's pre-stroke abilities remained a mystery to me until I'd been living with brain injury for about seven years. That's when I finally realized why my life lacks the smooth flow it once had. My brain no longer automatically processes information captured by my five senses. It simply files the information away somewhere and goes about the business of keeping me alive. Not that I'm complaining, mind you; I'm incredibly grateful to be alive.

I do, however, sometimes miss the higher-level cognitive skills and automatic connections between brain and body I relied on pre-stroke. In

Gee, I wish… …I'd been more patient, with myself and others.

particular, I miss my ability to accurately detect sounds, understand and retain spoken words, multi-task, store information in my short-term memory, and think on my feet.

A few years back, I decided these skills probably won't be *spontaneously* returning and started figuring out ways to compensate for them. This chapter describes some of the different habits and processes I've adopted to accommodate my stroke-modified life.

Higher-level cognitive skills give people the ability to plan, solve problems, control impulses, see how bits of information fit together, inhibit inappropriate behavior, think creatively, and simultaneously see both the big picture and underlying details. As with all thinking abilities, some people have better higher-level cognitive skills than others, just like some people are good at math while others are good with words.

Living with my diminished higher-level cognitive skills is incredibly challenging and frustrating, for me and (probably) for my loved ones. Missteps in behavior are very difficult to preempt so generally they come to my attention only after I've made a *bad choice*. Often, someone affected by my misstep is the one who brings it to my attention because I don't automatically notice how my actions affect others.

To avoid dwelling on the past, I'll simply say that on a scale of 1-to-10 (1 = awful and 10 = awesome) I'd rate my higher-level cognitive skills as at least a nine before my stroke and maybe a three, these days.

My ability to quickly grasp the big picture and think through the details needed to bring it to life helped me excel in life without much effort, pre-stroke. As an added bonus, I could effectively multi-task. For example, in my pre-stroke communications job, I'd actively participate in emotionally charged, 3-hour meetings with company leaders and my communications peers while taking clear, concise notes; developing a communication plan; and drafting key pieces of that plan.

When these meetings adjourned, I'd have an action plan ready to implement and would have most of the supporting communications materials ready for review. Anything I hadn't written during the meeting was listed in the plan with my notes available for another communicator to use for reference. I didn't need them because anything I needed to remember was carefully filed away in my brain.

- Productive? Yes.
- Rewarding? Yes.
- Controlling? Highly.
- Tiring? Yes.
- Process-driven? No.

My approach to work wasn't particularly healthy, but it did make good use of my multi-tasking ability, a skill which seems critical to worldly success. Perhaps that's why so many people risk life and limb talking on a cell phone, applying make-up, or reading while driving. Back then, I figured if success required multi-tasking, I'd just out multi-task everyone else.

That thinking changed when my right middle cerebral artery ruptured. My *bleed* killed an unknown number of cells in various parts of my brain. None of those cells was needed to keep me alive, but some must have helped direct my higher-level cognitive skills.

While under Dr. Lee's care at the Center, he'd predicted these skills had been compromised by my stroke, but I didn't realize what he meant for about seven years. He was right; my old work style had been quite dependent on my higher-level cognitive skills. Okay… so it took a while for me to figure that out. Let's just say it's tough to think through how your thinking has been rearranged after your thinking gets rearranged. There's some good irony…

Assorted comments others had made about my behavior, word choice, appearance, expression, etc. since my stroke all made sense when I finally connected them with Dr. Lee's input about impaired higher-level cognitive skills. There's a familiar image of a light bulb coming on above a person's head when he gets a bright idea. To me, the realization of how stroke had impacted these skills was like standing in the middle of Yankee Stadium in the evening wearing a blindfold. Suddenly, someone walked up behind me and ripped the blindfold from my face, exposing me to a painfully bright light, with thousands of people staring at me.

After realizing I have an invisible disability which had prompted some unusual behaviors, I was able to take a critical first step toward recovery. The fix was obvious. I *simply* needed to relearn my higher-level cognitive skills. It didn't take long for me to realize that's easier said than done. Near as I can tell, a person is born with or without these skills. Those born with strong higher-level cognitive skills, then have the opportunity to hone them throughout life.

This is comparable to either being good or not-so-good at math. My high school math teacher, Ted, could confirm I'm in the latter category. God designed my brain to excel with words and images, not numbers. Even if I could **bear** to study math for the rest of my life, I wouldn't be good at it on my death-bed. God also gifted me with strong higher-level cognitive skills. However, some of the brain cells needed to employ those skills died on Jan. 30, 2000, and aren't coming back.

To adapt to my new situation, I decided to identify processes that would enable me to respond to events in my life as if I understood what was happening. These processes would help me to make sense of events that my brain didn't *put together* as it had pre-stroke. For example, if someone asks me a question that really floors me, I've trained myself to first respond, "Tell me where you heard that." The brief interlude provided by the background he provides, gives me time to decide if I can answer the question on the spot or should defer answering until I've had time to pull my thoughts together.

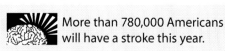 More than 780,000 Americans will have a stroke this year.

This process worked well when one of the boys asked me if I'd ever heard of an infamous serial killer. Although I hadn't heard the man's name in years, the question brought back a flood of unpleasant memories. As our son described how the name had been used on the school playground, I ran the following process through my mind:

1. Is he old enough for a candid answer? If not, go to step 2; if so, go to step 3.

2. Answer a related question I wish he'd have asked.

3. Think through the correct explanation and identify three talking points to follow. For this question, my talking points were:

   a. He was a young man who kidnapped, tortured, and killed little boys.

   b. He was convicted for those murders and sent to prison.

   c. He can never hurt you because the other inmates killed him as soon as he was admitted.

4. Remind myself to stick to my talking points and start talking.

My talking points were then recycled as I responded to the usual litany of "but why would…" questions that followed. I keep this process posted in a kitchen cupboard for easy reference. When I don't have time to prepare talking points, I think of a verse of Scripture related to the topic at-hand. Who can argue with God's word? This approach accommodates my higher-level cognitive skill challenges and shows Troy, Trent, and Don how the Gospel applies to daily living.

Given that I now spend time reading the Bible each day, more Scripture verses are becoming available in my long-term memory, which is a big help.

Although it's best to read scripture verses in context, there are times when I rely on a verse or two to help address situations where Trent, Don, and I are driving one another crazy. This process begins with me taking a time-out to find a relevant verse and think through how I should share it with the boys. Next, I tell Trent and Don to meet me in the living room with their Bibles. I prefer to read the King James Version of the Bible, since it's been interpreted by fewer people than other versions. However, hearing how different authors have rewritten a verse does sometimes help me develop my understanding of it.

After each boy reads the verse from his Bible, we discuss it to see how our behavior is or isn't fitting God's plan for us. For example, after hearing someone yell, "I hate you!" from the room where Trent and Don were *playing*, we read 1 John 4:20 together. In the KJV of the Bible, this verse says, "If a man say, I love God, and hateth his brother, he is a liar: for he that loveth not his brother whom he hath seen, how can he love God whom he hath not seen?"

It's pretty clear how this verse relates to the shouting I overheard so I had to discipline myself to let the verse speak for itself.

AUTO-PILOT IS OFF

I've had to figure out ways to help overcome the fact my brain no longer consistently communicates basic needs to my body. For example, to avoid overeating or passing out due to lack of nourishment, I eat the same types of food, in the same quantity, at the same time every day. Even when Troy takes our family out to eat, I order something as similar as possible to what I would have eaten at home. My nutrition process compensates for the fact I don't automatically feel hunger pangs.

GOOD FOOD, GONE BAD AND *BAD* GONE GOOD

I've also needed some changes in my diet post-stroke. Chocolate now does something very weird to my brain. Although I've never used any illegal drug, I think my reaction to chocolate is comparable to being high. Once, after drinking a glass of chocolate-flavored soy milk, I blanked out for about three hours. One minute I was sitting in our home drinking the milk, and the next I was sitting in a meeting at our church. I looked at familiar faces to my left and right, saw our pastor sitting across from me, and said, "Hi."

Everyone chuckled and our pastor said, "Hi, E; how ya doing?" When I asked if I'd been there long, someone said it had been about an hour. Apparently I'd been involved in the discussion our team was having and had even made some rather useful suggestions. I sat through the rest of the meeting wondering whether I'd driven or walked to the meeting, and trying to identify what might have caused this unusual situation. After our closing prayer, I walked outside and saw my car parked in its usual spot. When I got home, I told Troy what had happened, and he asked what I'd had for supper.

As I told him how chocolate-flavored soy milk tastes almost as good as the vanilla-flavor I usually bought, I got a hunch I knew what had happened. I wasn't willing to remove chocolate from my diet without proof, however, so I did a taste test about a week later. One small square of chocolate sent me to la-la land for about 45 minutes. My reaction to beer is very similar, so I no longer consume any form of chocolate or any alcoholic beverage.

Although I've not heard of similar reactions to food or drink among other stroke survivors, I did ask a neurologist about my sensitivity to chocolate. He'd heard about similar reactions in other brain injury survivors and in children living with ADHD.

Fortunately, I can still drink coffee…in small doses. I used to be a pot-a-day kind of gal but now limit myself to two cups each morning. Ironically, if I have too much coffee, it puts me to sleep. Yes. You read that correctly. Too much coffee puts me to sleep. And, I never, ever put sugar in my coffee or my brain shuts down. The same concept applies to sodas. If I drink a caffeinated soda, it has to be artificially sweetened or I'm out like a light. Sugar can also cause problems for me in the absence of caffeine. Through trial-and-error, I've learned my brain can tolerate up to 11 grams of sugar at a time. Kind of crazy, isn't it?

> Our eyes can fully attend to one thing at a time because both eyes communicate with the same brain, which is designed to attend to one thing at a time. The same is true of our ears.

There are a few items I've added to my post-stroke diet, too. For starters, I eat prunes every day. I hadn't even tasted a prune until my time in the Center, where I had to eat at least seven a day to help keep me regular. Apparently there was enough fiber in those withered plums to help even when the left half of my large intestine was paralyzed. After eating the *prescribed* dose of prunes each day for six and a half years, my gut mysteriously woke-up.

But, as a creature of habit, I still eat prunes every day…usually seven, of course. On a more exciting note, I can now eat many spicy foods. Having been raised in a home where spices (including salt and pepper) weren't used to cook anything, I reached adult-hood as a spice wimp. However, since the left half of my tongue is on limited speaking terms with my brain, I can chew spicy foods on that side of my mouth and enjoy the flavor without breaking into a cold sweat. I do have to be extra careful when chewing gum or my left cheek may become an unwilling chew toy as I lose track of where it is, relative to the teeth on my left side.

For some odd reason, my brain now seems to be protein-dependent. I assume this need is due to my brain injury, given I didn't need to pay attention to my protein intake pre-stroke. To keep it in full working order, I consume what I consider an inordinate amount of protein each day. I have at least 11 grams of protein at breakfast, lunch, and supper. Some people look for calories on food labels; I look for protein content.

To avoid getting dehydrated, I drink water throughout each day. My goal is to drink at least a gallon a day. This approach also solves the problem of me not automatically feeling the need to take a bio break. When my water cups are empty, I go refill them and notice there's a restroom nearby. This habit has become a handy way to kill two birds with one stone.

Time Always Flies

My tendency to lose track of time isn't linked only with what I consume. It seems the internal clock I used to rely on was short-circuited by my stroke. I recall, in the past, having a pretty good sense of how much time had passed between events in my life. For example, when making spaghetti, I'd automatically know how long the water had been boiling and know when to remove the pan. Now, I have no idea how long it's been boiling and may turn the stove off when the noodles are still crunchy or when they've assumed the consistency of glue.

To handle this challenge, I rely on my watch's timer to keep track of time. It's an easy fix, which I employ probably 15 times in an average day. My watch also has an alarm, which I use to remind myself of my next time commitment. For example, although I wake-up at about 4:15 each morning, my alarm sounds at 6:21

a.m., just in case. After getting up, I may reset the alarm to remind me of an appointment at 9:30. While at that appointment, I may reset it to make sure I drop one of the boys off at practice at 4 p.m. During practice, it's reset again to remind me of a 6:30 meeting.

A Place for Everything

Troy's been instrumental in helping me learn to live with my post-stroke organization challenges. He's one of those a place-for-everything and everything-in-its-place kind of people. In contrast, I was born a packrat extraordinaire. My ability to visualize which pile I put something in made this tendency tolerable to me, before my stroke. Since visualizing anything is quite taxing now, *glumping* like items in a pile is no longer a good approach to organizing.

Old habits die hard, but I eventually got tired of sorting through my clutter trying to find something I needed and decided to adopt Troy's approach to organization. Dad provides the motivation I need to keep sorting, recycling, and filing. My pack-ratting tendency comes from him, and I don't want to confront the same type of challenge Dad did when he moved to a senior housing facility. He'd saved everything of *value* during his 46 years in my childhood home and stored it in the house or barn.

The immediate benefits of my new approach to organization include being able to quickly find what I need, which saves time, reduces frustration, and helps keep my mind organized. I still have a few *mountains* of stuff to sort through, as time permits.

One aspect of Troy's organizing scheme doesn't suit my needs, however. If everything must be in its place at all times, I often forget to take things with me when I leave home. To accommodate my memory challenges, I tend to put items I need to take with me where I must step over them as I leave. Troy may think it odd to see an empty syrup bottle on the floor near the front door, but it works for me. I've learned that for this approach to be effective, I need to tell him what item is where it doesn't belong, and ask him to leave it alone.

Keeping Myself Vertical

I've also modified some old habits for safety's sake since my memory isn't as sharp as I'd like, and my brain no longer auto-matically communicates with some parts of my body. For example, although I can still ride a bicycle, I don't because it takes so much mental energy to keep the bike balanced, I'm unable to keep track of traffic and other hazards.

Flip-flop footwear is also a thing of the past for me. This open-to-the-air style has some appeal during summers in the Midwest but they wreak havoc with my balance. Seems my brain doesn't understand the messages my feet send it and I get all tangled up in the flipping and flopping.

While at the Center, I learned to drain the bathtub before getting out so at least I wouldn't drown if I slipped and fell.

MEMORY

Unlike many stroke survivors, I don't need any medicines to prevent a recurrent stroke. However, I do take a couple of prescription medicines and over-the-counter medicines. For these, I now use a pillbox rather than relying on my memory to open an assortment of individual containers each morning or evening. Both my morning and evening pillbox have enough compartments to last a month.

ACHES AND PAINS

I'm not able to gauge the importance of any pain I happen to feel since my stroke. When I notice a mysterious ache or pain, I get Troy's opinion on what might be wrong. For example, when I couldn't figure out why my right foot was hurting, Troy suggested I might be tying my shoe too tightly. At first I was mildly offended by his response but then decided to loosen the lace. By golly, he was right! I also ask his opinion if my left arm or leg (my affected side) is numb.

As you might imagine, having had a hemorrhage in the right side of my brain causes me to get a bit *wiggy* when I have **any** pain on that side of my head. My process for handling that type of pain is to pray, run through the stroke warning signs in my mind, and ask Troy if he's noticed any *odd* behavior on my part.

He's very good about reminding me it's perfectly normal for me to get a minor headache and that I'm still prone to sinus infections. Since he's the only one who remembers how much pain I was in just before my stroke, I rely on his opinion when he says a headache isn't something I should worry about.

I follow a similar process when one of our sons has a headache. They may be the only youngsters in our area whose mom ticks off the stroke warning signs to help them feel better but when a child knows Mom almost died after having a really bad headache, you *go with what you know.*

Over time, I realized my affected (left) side is a good predictor of my health. When I'm getting ill, my left arm and leg generally feel numb the day before more *typical* symptoms surface. For example, one evening I told Troy I thought I was getting a cold. He asked a logical triage question, "Is your throat sore?" and looked at me rather oddly when I said, "No, but my left arm has been numb all day." For some reason, my response didn't make sense to him. As if having a numb arm is unrelated to having a cold… I could barely croak, "See… I told you I was getting a cold," when he asked how I was feeling the next morning.

MRS. NO-DEPTH PERCEPTION

Initially, it was tough for me to park in our garage due to unreliable depth perception. Inevitably, I'd pull forward too far and bump the shelves, a bike, or the trash container. If I didn't pull forward far enough, the garage door would nail my back bumper. To solve this challenge, I positioned my car in the correct spot, attached a piece of string to the ceiling with a thumb tack, and cut the string where it brushed the windshield. Next, I attached a paper clip to the string so it *clinks* when it bumps the windshield.

AN ORGANIZED MIND

Good organization skills also help the brain process information it receives. It's very difficult for me, post-stroke, to filter information and retain only what is or may be important for future use. To accommodate this challenge, I'm very particular about what information I allow to enter my mind. I don't watch TV or read the newspaper, and listen only to Christian radio stations. Rather than interrupting my focus by answering the phone, I often let the answering machine pick-up.

If I absorbed every bit of information cast my way each day, my brain would be full of bits of information with nothing linking them together and, therefore, no relevance. This *isolation* approach works for me because I hear about what's relevant to our life from Troy, at the Y, or through church friends. Sure… I'm occasionally surprised to hear news that everyone's been talking about for ages but oh well. As long as I can keep track of what affects our family, *I'm good.*

THINKING

I've learned to give myself time to *think on things* overnight. During the day there are so many distractions it's often difficult for me to think through an important topic. By intentionally remembering what I need to think about just before falling asleep, I often awaken with the answer I need.

This approach also helps address my tendency to *churn*, or perseverate. It can be difficult for me to stop thinking about one topic and move onto the next. When I find myself churning about something, I can often clear my head by taking a nap.

Life is less spontaneous than it was when I thought I was immortal. The good news is that I have enough brain cells left to make up for many of the deficits my stroke created. Life may flow more smoothly for someone whose brain automatically hears what her body is telling her and whose body obeys her brain, but I get by. Although it often feels like someone has submerged my head in gelatin, I make the most of each day I have here on Earth.

One sticking point is that life is unpredictable. No matter how good my processes are or how many processes I develop, there are challenges each day. My definition of multi-tasking has shifted from the emotion-laden meeting described earlier to the *challenge* of making a grilled cheese sandwich while carrying on a conversation.

The trade-offs I live with are fine by me, because my brain keeps my heart beating and my lungs inhaling and exhaling. For a while,

I longed to be care-free, independent, and *in-control* like I was before my stroke, then I saw how God works in mysterious ways to maintain fellowship with me.

I didn't choose to rely on God the first 33 years of my life but He was there waiting for me when I finally turned to Him for the boundless love and wisdom only He can provide. God and I are in constant conversation now, as I face each day of unknown joys and challenges. The only process I've found which covers every challenge I encounter in this world is to turn it over to God in prayer.

Richard Nixon died of stroke at 81, some 20 years after resigning as President of the United States.

CHAPTER 12

IT IS WHAT IT IS

Stroke completely revamped my life, but you probably wouldn't know that just by looking at me. If we struck up a conversation, however, you'd start to notice the impact of my cognitive (AKA invisible) deficits. That's because the brain controls a person's ability to express emotions at the right time, and at an appropriate *level*, as surely as it directs the mouth to speak or an arm to move. These *glitches* are readily apparent only to me and a few others, such as Troy, who knew me well pre-stroke. Most of the adults I knew pre-stroke, save family members, faded out of my life. Only recently, did I realize my cognitive deficits may be what pushed them away.

Bottom line: My mind now works in mysterious ways — mysterious to others and to me.

My stroke prompted me to begin interacting with others as if I were about 14. After my stroke, I re-entered the world an opinionated, staunchly independent, and somewhat unpredictable character housed in an adult body. Early in my recovery, my injured brain's *performance* reminded me of the chaos it went through during puberty. My

Gee, I wish… …I'd willingly cleared the clutter from my mind.

early recovery was a lot like going through my teen years again at age 33. All it took to reset my social skills to those of a young teen was a small hole in my right middle cerebral artery and a heartbeat, which flooded my brain with blood.

These changes in my thinking don't present an immediate danger to anyone, but they've certainly skewed my view of the world. Most of them are merely irritations, but others have the potential to squelch significant relationships, if not managed well. Three of my deficits (vision, memory, and verbosity) are so annoying they earned separate chapters. Before I tell you about a few of the less bothersome ones, here's a snapshot of how post-stroke fatigue impacts my life.

For starters, every stroke survivor I know battles fatigue. This fatigue is unlike anything I experienced pre-stroke, including finals week in college and every phase of pregnancy. Unfortunately, it won't end with an exciting event, such as summer break or a baby; it just goes on and on. My fatigue even seems to intensify as my recovery progresses and I push myself to do more.

This tired feeling is a familiar side-effect of stroke, but isn't well-understood. It's so common among brain injury survivors that the staff at the Center thought to include a 45-minute nap in my schedule each afternoon before I even moved in. They also helped ensure I got eight to ten hours of sleep each night. Living with a brain injury in the *real world* is much more tiring than life at a rehab center. These days, I try to get at least ten hours of sleep each night and nap about three hours a day.

My theory about post-stroke fatigue is that when a person's brain gets injured, it focuses on doing required activities, such as breathing and circulating blood. To conserve energy, it may no longer automatically perform optional activities, such as chatting or keeping track of time. A survivor may still be able to handle these, and other, elective activities by deliberately *activating* them.

This change in approach reminds me of driving a manual transmission car after being accustomed to an automatic. Most of the equipment is the same but the mode of operation is different, requiring more energy and closer attention. As I see it, my surviving

brain cells work like they did pre-stroke, but some of the neurological connections needed for them to work together got snapped. As
a result, many of my higher-level cognitive skills got short-circuited
on Jan. 30, 2000. These missing connections require me to deliberately jump-start cognitive skills that used to deploy automatically.

Remembering to pace myself throughout each day has been
challenging as I make accommodations to get the best from what's
left of my brain. In the past, I'd get a bit spacey when overly tired,
but now I can almost **feel** my mind shutting down. If I push myself
too hard and ignore my need for rest and relaxation, my thinking abilities shut down and my body crashes in exhaustion. It also
takes a lot longer for me to recuperate than it did pre-stroke. The
thought of studying all night, a frequent occurrence in college, is
unimaginable to me now.

Piecing bits of information together to form a smooth flow of
ideas is so tiring I sometimes crash even when well-rested. This
challenge first become apparent in cognitive therapy sessions that
left me so drained I was fearful of driving myself home. Making
cognitive connections in the real world is even more tiring and difficult. After focusing on a challenging task, I sleep for an hour or
so before moving on to something else.

I've learned to take a break when my mind tells me to, no matter
what time that *nudge* comes. This aspect of my recovery reminds
me of how a baby learns and grows. A baby naturally needs lots of
sleep because she's growing and changing so quickly. Besides, this
world is as overwhelming to her as it is to me. When a baby gets
tired or overwhelmed, she sleeps. If you've been in a grocery store
in the early afternoon, you've probably heard what it's like when
a baby is forced to stay awake during her naptime. **Not** a pleasant
sound.

Post-stroke fatigue may not be an actual deficit, but rather the
result of living with an injured brain in an overwhelming world.

As mentioned earlier, the brain is the only body part physically
injured by stroke. Many limitations of stroke are, however, visible
to others. If the brain no longer communicates with an arm or leg,
for example, others can tell that limb no longer works. Although

it's probably fine physically, the brain no longer tells it what to do so it remains still. With a cognitive deficit, both physical injury to the brain and the challenges it creates are unseen because they affect *only* how the survivor thinks.

The **action** a survivor takes as a result of a cognitive challenge may affect others, however. For example, if I convince myself I can drive for three hours straight, there will likely be an accident because I'm pretty sure I'd fall asleep at the wheel. In that situation, several lives could be affected by the cognitive deficits which led me to overestimate my abilities.

Let's just say that my cognitive challenges provide new insight on the saying *rearranging deck chairs on the Titanic*. With that background, here's a quick look at some cognitive deficits which now haunt my life. These comments aren't intended to be medically accurate because I'm not a doctor. Each of them is what it is, and I've come to believe that what's most important for me is to minimize the impact each has on my life.

Who am I and what am I doing here? — The cells that got scrambled in my right hemisphere obviously helped me keep track of my place in the universe because I now struggle to keep track of where I fit in the big picture and to understand what's expected of me. This vexing deficit limits my ability to see things about myself which are painfully obvious to others. It also makes it tough to identify and manage my other deficits. Basically, I tend to think the way I do things is perfectly *normal* while those around me wonder how many times they'll have to tell me it's aberrant.

This disconnect happens because I don't absorb and process information the same way as others. As a result, I don't see their point. If my approach works for me, I don't see why it should bother anyone else.

Being unaware of my abilities and challenges led to some interesting therapy sessions, soon after my stroke. When I started walking again, for example, I twisted my knee when a physical therapist asked me to stand up after doing floor exercises. I vaguely recall being insulted she'd ask me to do something so simple and decided to get up quickly to show her I didn't need her help. Not a good idea. My legs twisted into a crumpled pile under me as I fell to the floor.

The impact of not fully comprehending how I should and shouldn't behave in public is more subtle, and difficult to accommodate. For example, I used to carry my *purse stuff* in a gardener's vest to eliminate the risk of forgetting my purse somewhere. This handy garment had so many pockets I could *wear* anything I might need when out and about.

This solution worked well during the winter but when summer arrived, Troy pointed out it was a bit odd to wear an extra layer to our son's baseball games. To me, it made perfect sense to wear my vest because the risk of leaving my purse at a game seemed so real. I figured he'd get over it and continued wearing my vest. Surely he was exaggerating how the world views my appearance, right?

To Troy's advantage, however, a kid in Don's acting class asked him, "Is your dad in the Army?" while he was standing next to me. When Don asked for clarification, the kid pointed to my vest. Apparently it made me look rather masculine, and the kid thought it held some sort of weapon or ammo. When a total stranger (a child, at that) thinks I dress strangely, I pay attention. My gardener's vest now resides next to the fanny pack I wore earlier in my recovery. I retired that memory aid when someone at work politely mentioned most women my age carry a purse, rather than wearing a fanny pack.

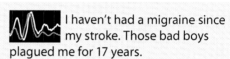 I haven't had a migraine since my stroke. Those bad boys plagued me for 17 years.

One bugaboo of this deficit is that it leaves loved ones, usually a stroke survivor's best source of honest feedback, as the ones most likely to be ignored. Worse yet, they're the easiest to blame when something goes wrong in a survivor's life. I tend to blame Troy, Trent, or Don for something before considering the fact I may be the one who screwed up. When you're only marginally aware of your own existence and what you're doing, it's easier to see problems in someone else. If you or someone you love is recovering from a brain injury, you might consider discussing the potential impact of this challenge with a qualified counselor.

Where am I?—In addition to not understanding where I philosophically fit in the universe, I tend to also get lost physically. This may be because the right side of the brain equips a person to stay oriented, gauge distance, estimate size and speed, determine an object's location, and figure out how pieces fit together to make a whole. Some common challenges linked with this loss were mentioned earlier.

Odd Social Behavior—It was rather unnerving to realize, about six years post-stroke, I'd been acting like someone whose brain is undergoing the changes associated with puberty. Like a young teen, I'd been acting impulsively, thinking the universe revolved around me, struggling to interact appropriately with others, and seeing the world in black and white, rather than shades of grey. The catch is that most people expect a woman who looks *normal* to act her age.

Although I look fairly *normal*, at least by my definition, if we struck-up a conversation, you'd probably soon realize I'm not your ordinary, average Jo. You might find my body language a bit unusual. Perhaps I'd stand too near you sometimes, at other times, too far away. You'd probably wonder why I seem unsure what to do with my hands. You might even notice my posture sometimes belies my mood. Perhaps I slouch while talking excitedly or stand bolt upright while talking softly.

Pre-stroke, those who knew me well might have described me as candid, tactful, empathetic, and predictable. Folks are more apt to say I'm blunt, insensitive, egocentric, and surprising these days. Any description of my post-stroke style would vary widely depending on the weather, date and time, setting, how I'm feeling, and the price of eggs, however, because my mind and behavior are now easily affected by external stimuli.

My cognitive (and therefore social) skills work just fine if I can plan ahead and if I stay focused. Those are two mighty-big ifs, however, because social interactions are often impromptu. Without a plan to execute, there's really no point in my staying focused so it's anybody's guess how I'll respond. When caught off-guard, I often try to distract those around me with humor while collecting my thoughts.

Someday I may be able to rely on nonverbal communication rather than humor again, but I think that's going to take some time. These skills enable a person to make appropriate expressions and stand in a way that conveys appropriate meaning. The brain's right hemisphere handles these skills, however, so mine took a hit when my brain hemorrhaged. On the flip side, I also tend to overlook or misread others' nonverbal cues.

If you could observe me in my natural habitat, our home, you'd eventually notice some other childish traits. Troy, Trent, and Don usually treat me as a *normal* adult, but sometimes they baby me. Let me assure you, they do this in response to my behavior, not because they occasionally forget I'm *the mom*. Like a young teen, I prefer the adult treatment until something intimidates or scares me, then it's back to being a child. This switch usually happens when I get overwhelmed.

In other words, I expect others to treat me as a fully capable adult until something freaks me out, then I want to be babied. How are they supposed to know which hat I'm wearing? Can you imagine how awkward it must be for my husband to treat me like a delinquent teen or for one of our sons to reprimand me? Who's raising whom? Haven't I been through this before? Sure I have, but my first experience with becoming independent was in the late 1970s.

The teen years must also naturally include the tendency to be impulsive, egocentric, and overly confident because I struggled mightily with these as I started my second trip through puberty. For example, each person has a different comfort zone for sharing and hearing personal information. Our sons learned in school to think of this zone as their *personal bubble*. Apparently, my stroke expanded the diameter of my *personal bubble*, because, early on, I shared more personal information than warranted in casual conversations.

Accepting Jesus Christ as my Lord and Savior immediately cured me of my *Center of the Universe Syndrome* and I expect my savoir faire to continue improving as I remain focused on things above, not on the earth. There's simply too much sinning going on down here for this mind to handle.

Emotional—It's a good thing I don't embarrass easily, because I now tend to cry unpredictably and with little provocation. Although I've always been outspoken and animated, my ability to appropriately express emotions was affected by my stroke. For example, I'd automatically sob if anything went wrong the first few years of my recovery. These *floods* seemed to bother others more than me. I'd simply locate some tissue, remind myself to think through the situation, and realize 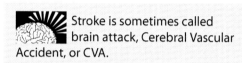 Stroke is sometimes called brain attack, Cerebral Vascular Accident, or CVA. (nine times out of ten) it didn't warrant tears.

This problem, called *emotional lability* among the medical crowd, is the result of physical changes in the brain impacting how a person handles her emotions. Every brain injury survivor I know struggles with expressing emotions appropriately, regardless of how their injury was sustained.

A greater challenge of my rampant emotions is impaired anger management, which became apparent when I moved back home. Living in this world is much more challenging than living within the safe confines of a rehab center. Not that I'd fly into a fit of rage, but it didn't take much to aggravate me, and it took a long time for me to calm down.

At this point in my recovery, I've accepted the fact that my emotions may not become more predictable, but I'm okay with that. Tempering one's emotions must be at least partially a learned skill because I do feel more prepared to handle emotionally charged situations as my mind matures again. Besides, I'd rather display too much emotion than too little.

Connecting the Dots—Many everyday situations require a person to piece together bits of disparate information to draw a logical conclusion. This problem-solving ability requires the right and left hemispheres of our brain to work together. Grasping the *big picture* is mostly a right hemisphere skill; identifying the details needed to construct that picture is mostly left-hemisphere stuff. The two hemispheres of our brain work together courtesy of a group of nerve fibers called the corpus callosum.

My ability to draw logical conclusions is noticeably impaired so I assume my corpus callosum was compromised by stroke. In fact, it's so hard for me to figure out what a bunch of details might mean, that I often discuss a mundane situation with a trusted friend who helps me figure out what I'm describing. Only then can I start breaking it down into the details needed to move ahead.

Distractibility—The most challenging cognitive loss I've identified in myself, to date, is *distractibility*. This annoyance includes a short attention span, limited ability to multi-task, getting distracted easily, making rough transitions among tasks, and, as a result, getting overwhelmed easily. This deficit is quite trying because our world moves at a frenetic pace, as you know. I focus lots of energy accommodating for my distractibility because personal safety is critical.

Pre-stroke, few things could distract me from the task-at-hand, as I automatically ignored stimuli that didn't warrant my attention. With that automatic filtering process gone, I now get distracted easily.

This is partially due to the fact my brain attends to any interesting, unexpected, or repetitive noise. Red lights are also highly distracting. When driving, if I pass a police car stopped on the shoulder with its lights on, it takes a lot of effort for me not to get almost hypnotized by the lights. To avoid getting mesmerized, I deliberately focus on the center line and pretend my peripheral vision is temporarily out-of-order.

This overstimulation leaves me unable to decipher what should get my attention, and my mind reacts by quickly switching its focus. As a result, it's tough for anything to get my undivided attention.

This cognitive challenge helped me realize multi-tasking isn't necessarily a good practice. When I try to focus on multiple activities, I get impulsive, tending to jump to conclusions and think I know what's going on, when in reality, I haven't a clue. As an alternative, I sometimes focus on one detail and beat it to death, ignoring all others.

Avoidance helps somewhat with my inability to *shift gears* smoothly. Troy, Trent, and Don know I'm waving the white surrender flag when I say, "I can only do 14 things at a time!" This comment usually comes when more than one of them is firing questions at me or someone asks a *tricky*, compound question, such as, "Are we staying home for supper tonight or going out for pizza?"

The old phrase *shifting gears* refers to a person's ability to transfer her attention among activities. My mind used to automatically gravitate toward whatever activity deserved my closest attention. After sizing-up that activity, it would automatically move on to the next most important thing. Those days are gone. My mind now tends to get sucked in by whatever first gets its attention. Any activity that involves an interesting **sound** generally gets top priority.

There may be other, more important events going on in the general vicinity, but until I consciously tell my mind to close the gate on the sound and open another gate, my world revolves around the sound that captured my attention. In addition, any shift in my focus is pretty rough. It's like one large, iron gate slams shut and another one clangs open against a brick wall.

This challenge is probably the result of my injured brain's inability to multi-task. If a familiar task has my undivided attention, I can accomplish it pretty well. If my attention is divided among two or more tasks, however, things can get ugly quickly. That's because if my attention is divided among multiple activities, none of them gets my best effort.

One example of the dangers of distractibility and multi-tasking is cell phone use while driving. I didn't understand why so many people thought this was dangerous until I started driving again post-stroke. Now that driving safely requires my undivided attention, I get it. I think the dangers introduced by cell phone usage while driving are primarily the result of the driver trying to concentrate on multiple activities. The simple fact is that if the driver's mind is focused on having a meaningful conversation with the person on the other end of the phone, she isn't fully focused on driving safely. Conversely, if she's focused on driving safely, she probably isn't having a truly meaningful conversation.

Of course, these distracting conversations can just as easily be held with someone who's in the car. I sometimes ask our sons to sit silently until a tense driving situation is past. Meaningful conversations can also be distracting in other situations. One day I torched two grilled cheese sandwiches beyond recognition while talking with Don. We were running late for something so I threw the sandwiches on to cook while Don told me about his day at school. We tend to have fairly animated conversations so I wasn't too shocked when he informed me the sandwiches were smoking. Ever optimistic, I flipped them over thinking I'd cook the other side, peel off the charred parts, and have plenty left for Don to eat. Then it was back to our conversation, until he announced, "Mom, you did it again!" Sure enough, the opposite side of both sandwiches had gone up-in-flames. Oh well. At least I learned more about my multi-tasking challenge, in a safe environment.

The polar opposite of distractibility is perseveration, described earlier. Someone who perseverates is "like a dog with a bone." This challenge frustrates me because it's so difficult for me to shift gears. If there's anything worse than being unable to focus on what deserves my attention, it's being unable to shift my attention away from something that doesn't deserve it. For example, if someone asks me a question, it's a real struggle for me to continue participating in the conversation until I've answered it to my satisfaction, even if it's irrelevant to what we're discussing.

I've learned a lot about my cognitive deficits through therapy and counseling but my mind still surprises me on a regular basis. In many ways, it's like a house divided against itself. Matthew 12:25 tells us, "...Every kingdom divided against itself is brought to desolation; and every city or house divided against itself shall not stand." My right hemisphere is missing innumerable brain cells and no longer communicates with my left hemisphere as smoothly as it did pre-stroke. Ah well; it is what it is.

These deficits also seem to make it difficult for me to establish and maintain close, personal relationships, but God still loves me. He still loves you, too, even if you've yet to accept the sacrifice His

Son made on our behalf more than 2,000 years ago.

Although God's the only One who knows exactly how my post-stroke mind works, I have a pretty good handle on it, given I interact with it 24/7. Even with that advantage, it's a good thing I have the rest of my life to learn how to use my new brain, with its *Jesus piece* in place.

In addition to the challenges above, I should mention one major difference in my personality post-stroke. I now enjoy public speaking, something I avoided like the plague pre-stroke. The thought of addressing an audience terrified me, until my life experiences provided two topics so important they overtook that fear: living in relationship with God and stroke prevention.

Peggy Lee, American singer and actress, died of stroke at 81.

CHAPTER 13

BE STILL AND
KNOW HIM

Romans 3:23 says, "...all have sinned, and come short of the glory of God." This verse tells me there's no way anyone can **earn** a spot in Heaven. We humans simply aren't worthy to be in God's presence, because we're prone to sin. God created Adam and Eve as free-willed creatures and turned them loose in a paradise called the Garden of Eden.

Our tendency to sin was established when they ate fruit from the one tree in the Garden God specifically told them to leave alone. As Genesis 2:17 tells us, "But of the tree of the knowledge of good and evil, thou shalt not eat of it: for in the day that thou eatest thereof thou shalt surely die."

Adam and Eve didn't physically die after eating the forbidden fruit but being disconnected from God by sin caused them to spiritually die. Worse yet, their inability to resist Satan's temptation ensured all future humans would be susceptible to his wiles. All humans born since that moment have entered this world

Gee, I wish... ...I'd accepted Jesus as my Lord and Savior long before I did.

separated from God by sin, as a result. Being disconnected from our Creator causes a person to feel incomplete, in some way.

A newborn baby hasn't sinned, obviously, but she'll succumb to a temptation soon after learning to exercise her free will. Many people try to avoid sinning by relying on their conscience and upbringing, but the one way to consistently deny Satan is to have God's Holy Spirit on your side. That connection can be made only by realizing that Jesus Christ, the Son of God, the only sinless person to ever live, died and was resurrected so God will forgive your sins.

It took a massive stroke, and almost 40 years, for me to realize God's love is all I need to feel whole. Like most folks, I was focused on having it all, not realizing the mysterious *all* isn't what I need, anyway. My ability to resist temptation during that time came from the *clean living and right thinking* mentality my parents instilled in me. Now that I'm saved, God's Holy Spirit helps me resist temptation, even in my *altered* state of mind. He's ready, willing, and able to do the same for you, no matter who you are, what you've done, and what temptations you face.

> As a child, I had a wonderful place, under three huge evergreen trees in the far northeast corner of our acreage, where I felt incredibly close to God. I'd sit under their branches for hours, quietly considering life, my place in the world, and what happens to people when they die.

You may not recognize this emptiness in your soul until your life hits an extreme low point. My stroke was a low point in my life but my extreme low hit in the form of a massive depression, about six years later, when I began to realize how stroke had changed the way I understand information and communicate with others. The day that reality hit home is when I accepted the validity of what I'd read and heard about Jesus Christ dying so my sins would be forgiven.

Now I know my soul will one day enter Heaven to spend eternity with God. Better yet, whenever I ask God, "What's next, Lord?" His Holy Spirit provides the guidance I need. God doesn't control which step I take but rather helps me understand what I should do. He doesn't control the thoughts or actions of anyone. As I said earlier, sin has controlled this world since Eve fell for the enemy's lie in the Garden of Eden.

> **SideNote:** Only my heart and mind were transformed by the Holy Spirit's presence in me, but others soon noticed some positive changes in my priorities and in how I take care of my body, or as it's called in I Corinthians, my *temple*.

Relinquishing control over my life feels natural now that I know God isn't micro-managing it either. That realization came to me in a vision when I asked God why He *made* me have a stroke. What I immediately heard back from God is that He doesn't control what happens to me or anyone else. He is, however, constantly available to help us sort through the good, bad, and ugly events in our life.

It's no coincidence Trent asked me a couple of hours after this vision, "If God loves you so much, why'd He make you have a stroke? I mean, why does He even let bad things happen to good people?" I was able to say without hesitation, "God didn't make me have a stroke. He just made the most of a bad situation by being there when I opened my heart to accept the sacrifice Jesus Christ made for us more than 2,000 years ago."

Isn't it amazing our Father found a way to save us from ourselves? By offering His Son, Jesus Christ, as a sacrifice to atone for the sins all humans commit, God gave each person the option of escaping eternal damnation. Jesus' death and resurrection is the safety net that protects us from the sinful ways prompted by our free will. Knowing I'll spend eternity with God when I die enables me to remain calm and at peace in this world.

It wasn't long after the vision mentioned above that a girl in my Sunday School class left me momentarily speechless. That's tough to do but when Lindy asked me what God sounds like, I was a bit lost. Although I'd been in constant conversation with Him for quite some time by then, I tend to focus on **what** He says rather than **how** He says it. To buy myself some time, I asked Lindy to tell me what prompted her question.

Turns out Lindy was bummed that although she prays faithfully, she'd never heard anything back from God. That's when the answer hit me and I started to talk. Lindy and her classmates heard how I believe God speaks to each person in a way that works for that individual.

When I shared how God guides me through dreams, other believers, songs, Scripture verses, visions, a child's smile, even a cat's purr, the kids began to see how God's approach often doesn't require words. Given that God created everything, is it any wonder His creations speak on His behalf? Better yet, He seems to have infinite patience when it comes to getting, and keeping, our attention. God knocks on the door of your heart and then waits until you decide, of your own free will, to realize Jesus Christ died, was buried, and rose again so God would forgive us for our sins. (I Cor 15:1-4).

 One key to earning my BA in English and MA in journalism was my ability to ace essay tests. Such tests require the use of both brain hemispheres and smooth communication between the two. Something tells me I'd prefer multiple choice exams these days.

I've no doubt the Holy Spirit provided my response to Lindy's question because it had never crossed my mind, yet my answer was fluid, logical, and consistent with Scripture. If you're not quite ready to turn control of your life and eternal destiny over to God, you can still find reassurance of His power, love, and presence in Psalms 46, which glorifies God while providing a fair dose of solace for us.

God's in control of what becomes of this world in the long run and spells that out for us in the book of Revelation. The great unknown is the timing of those end-of-world events. You can be sure, however, that God will allow us to continue exercising our free will until He decides it's time for this earthly madness to end.

In some ways, my stroke made it easier for me to *be still* because my brain injury put an end to most non-essential thinking. My brain now operates short-handed, so it focuses on keeping life-sustaining systems going and spends little effort thinking about situations that **might** arise in the future. This change in my approach to thinking is fine by me. As I see it, stroke stilled my mind and provided the opportunity for God's love to fill my soul.

The enemy will use anything to try to distract you from being still. He may even tempt you to think good works can get you reconnected with God.

Losing your focus on things above won't cost you your spot in Heaven after you accept Jesus Christ as your Lord and Savior, but it may give the enemy some ammo. After all, what's an unsaved person likely to think if they see a Christian sin, break a law, or screw-up? He may tell himself, "If that's what a Christian is, I don't want to be like him." As a result, that soul and countless others may veer toward the enemy's side.

Although the Son is the only person of the Trinity (Father, Son, and Holy Ghost) who's been seen, seeing isn't *believing*, anyway. Seeing is *proving*. In contrast, *faith* is believing in what is unseen. I haven't seen God and don't plan to meet Him for many more years but I do know Him. In fact, I know Him better and better each day. My two main sources of information are the Bible and prayer. Hopefully, you have access to both of these sources, too. You can pray to God anytime. To build your prayers into a conversation, however, you must come to know Jesus Christ as your Lord and Savior.

You have the option of praying silently, even if you live somewhere prayer is forbidden. God knows every thought that passes through your mind, so you certainly don't need to pray aloud for His benefit.

If you struggle with the fact God is three people in one, you're not alone. Here's how I've explained Him to some confused souls:

Our home allows me to look over a ledge from the kitchen down into the living room. This vantage point comes in handy when I'm upstairs and our kids are downstairs. If things sound like they're getting out-of-hand, I look over the ledge to see what's up, hoping I don't have to go downstairs to straighten things out. Perhaps that's how God the Father views this world...

Generally, I catch myself thinking, "It may be time for me to go down there..." as I peer over the ledge. Can you imagine God reaching that conclusion before entering this world as a baby named Jesus?

When I make it down to our living room, I remind our sons how they're expected to behave, which reminds me of Jesus and His disciples teaching people how God expects them to live.

After *setting them straight*, I go back upstairs, leaving behind a new understanding—hopefully—of how they should behave, even when they can't see me. The expectations I leave with them remind me of how the Holy Spirit affects a saved person.

As you learn about God, you may find yourself wondering why more people haven't wiped their sin slate clean so they can walk through this life in peace. The answer may be that ever since Eve, and then Adam, broke God's one rule in the Garden of Eden, people have been focused on gaining more and more control over the world God gave us.

We've developed:

• Medicines to improve our length and quality of life;
• Transportation modes to take us across land and water, in record time;
• Ways to reach other planets and gaze into other galaxies;
• Methods for improving how we look and feel, and;
• Ways to control most of our surroundings, 24/7.

But have we mastered death? Studies show that ten out of ten people die someday, so why worry about that? You're still mortal, as am I, and when you die, your soul's eternal destination will be determined by whether or not you accepted the sacrifice made by a young Man you never saw in-the-flesh.

Stroke kills more women than men.

No amount of good works, time spent in house of worship, or dollars given to promote God's work could *earn* you a spot in Heaven. All you need to do is accept that God walked among us as Jesus Christ, endured all the mocking dished His way, died a torturous death on a Cross, and was resurrected.

Isn't it odd that although we haven't mastered death, many people still approach life as a race? Given that the goal of most races is to cross the finish line first (AKA die), what's the hurry? You have only from now until the day you die to get to know our Heavenly Father.

Although I've heard the saying, "Let Go and Let God" probably a thousand times, writing this chapter helped me assign meaning to it for the first time. It seems obvious to me now that it's based on what God tells us in Psalm 46:10, "Be still and know that I am God." When He spoke these words, God knew some human would *translate* them, hopefully in an effort to make them more meaningful to others. As is often the case, however, these translations have a different meaning than how God has led me to understand this verse. They also pack less of a punch than His Words.

Many parents use the words *be still* to hush a child. In that setting, it's clear the parent simply wants the child to be quiet. God probably has bigger expectations of us when He tells us to *be still* though. I think He's telling us to still our heart, mind, and body. Applying the phrase *be still* to these key elements of a human life requires much more effort than simply not talking. Basically, it requires her to relinquish the control she thinks she has over her own life.

Mary Todd Lincoln, President Abraham Lincoln's wife, died of stroke at 63.

CHAPTER 14

SOMEWHERE IN
MY MEMORY BANK

Many Americans spend lots of time and money preparing to die. Some buy a small plot of ground in a cemetery, usually near the grave of a loved one; others plan to be cremated. Do these preparations increase the chances a person will be remembered after they die? Probably. Would this time and money be better invested making memories with those they love?

I think so, because memories are important to most people. After all, each of us is the result of our experiences up to this point in our life. Said another way, memories of your past help define who you are right now. Today will soon be a part of that past, but you'll carry some memories of this day into the future.

Before I tell you how my memory got squelched by stroke, here's an overview of human memory, from my perspective. Imagine you have two memory *buckets* in your brain. The short-term memory bucket is a holding tank for information you'll probably need only in the here-and-now. Information you absorb through your five senses is dumped

Gee,
I wish...
...I'd learned to
listen to my body.

into this bucket where it remains available until you need it.

Its counterpart, the long-term memory bucket, stores information you should keep around for the long haul. One catch is that information can only enter long-term memory after being processed in short-term memory. Most likely, you'll use the information held in your short-term memory soon after it's processed. Then, if you probably won't need it again, you'll purge it. Some of that information will, however, be transferred from your short-term bucket to your long-term bucket for future use.

Remembering where you parked at the mall is an example of short-term information you should use and then purge. After all, you only need to know where you parked until you return to your car. That location is stored in short-term memory until you've found the car, then it's purged. In contrast, your home phone number was stored in short-term memory only until it was transferred to your long-term memory. You may have phone numbers from some previous residences stored in there, too. I still know my home phone number from 1972, thanks to my long-term memory.

All of this absorbing, processing, applying, purging, transferring, and retrieving of information is automatic for most folks. For those who've survived a brain injury, however, some or all of these cognitive activities may be impaired. Although my brain **can** still do most of these activities, some of them no longer happen automatically.

With those basics covered, here's some insight on how stroke impacted my memory. For starters, I have no memories from mid-December 1999 through mid-April 2000. Nothing. Zilch. Nada. In fact, the last pre-stroke memory I've pinned down for sure is the adoption of our cat, Puck. We have a picture of her labeled Nov. 27, 1999, so I know I'm remembering that correctly. I recall in great detail taking Trent to the local humane society and returning home with him and the cat.

Despite lots of research, I don't have a good explanation for why my long-term memory seems to have shut-down about six weeks before my stroke, which means I remember nothing about my 33rd birthday, Christmas of 1999, or anything else I experienced during those weeks. I generally video-tape our sons opening Christmas presents, however, and realized while at the Center I probably had a tape of our Christmas activities. Sure enough; the tape was still in our camcorder when I moved back home. I was optimistic there would be something on the tape to jog my memory of that day.

As the four of us watched the tape, I remembered each gift the boys opened. The expressions on their faces, however, were brand new to me. As usual, they seemed to like some of their gifts better than others. Why was I surprised by their reactions? Then it hit me. My Christmas shopping is usually done by Thanksgiving, so I'd purchased their gifts when my long-term memory was still *recording*. Between the buying and delivery, however, my memory shut-down. Ah well… at least I have the event on tape.

The medical folks who cared for me say I should be grateful to have no memory of the days leading up to my stroke because a brain hemorrhage is intensely painful. Although our brain doesn't experience pain itself, the blood vessels in the brain and surrounding membranes do. As I mentioned earlier, I thought the headache that started three days before my stroke was the worst migraine of my life.

Those same folks also told me that the better I got, the tougher my recovery would become. They weren't kidding. Relearning physical, occupational, speech, and recreational skills in therapy was nothing compared to realizing my short-term memory doesn't work like it used to. Although I get by pretty well (when I remember to use the memory aids I devised), my short-term memory sure isn't what it was pre-stroke.

It is much better than when I moved back home, at which time it was almost non-existent. Back then, if someone asked me what I'd eaten for breakfast, I couldn't remember whether or not I'd had breakfast, let alone what I ate. One glitch in this early phase of my recovery was brought to my attention by my sister-in-law, Carol, who pointed out I tended to remember every detail of a conversation except whom I talked with and/or whom we talked about. Forgetting key details isn't much better than having no memory at all.

Comparisons—My memory challenges are frustrating because I remember how well my memory worked pre-stroke. Although I often tell our sons, "Comparisons are nothing but hurtful," I find it difficult to not compare my pre-stroke and post-stroke memory. Perhaps that's because my diminished short-term memory seems to affect every waking moment of my life.

Another reason this comparison rears its ugly head is that I recall very clearly how well information in my long-term memory was organized before my stroke. It used to be easy for me to retrieve disparate bits of information about any topic I'd encountered in my first 33 years. Those memories must be etched in stone, like the Ten Commandments, because I can still access information from as far back as age five.

It sometimes takes awhile for me to retrieve information that's been filed away for decades, but I'm all right with that. When someone asks me something that taps into my long-term memory, I often say, "I'll think on it overnight." If I fall asleep thinking about that information, it generally surfaces by the following morning. One exception is my ability to almost instantaneously re-call the definition of words I haven't heard in years. 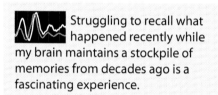 Struggling to recall what happened recently while my brain maintains a stockpile of memories from decades ago is a fascinating experience.

If I learned the meaning of a word years ago, I can retrieve it almost instantly, for some reason. It really comes in handy to have my vocabulary intact. When someone asks me what a word means, I simply need to hear how it's used in context, and the meaning comes to mind. For example, it took only a few seconds for me to recall *tintinnabulation* means *the ringing of bells*.

Naturally, some of the information stored in my long-term memory sometimes strikes another person as inaccurate. Given that most people probably trust their own memory, I have to be-lieve this would happen even if I hadn't had a stroke. When Troy and I talk about something from years ago and find we disagree about what really happened, we just agree to disagree. Each person stores memories based on his or her individual point of view, so it's no wonder we recall things differently.

Keeping my **short**-term memory in sync with Troy's is important, however. For example, if Troy asks me to pick Don up somewhere at six and my short-term memory *processes* seven, that's a problem. This type of miscommunication seldom happens because Troy's good about having me repeat back what I heard him say. He's also learned it's best to write down information I absolutely need to remember correctly. The handheld, digital recorder Troy got me also helps me keep track of whether I should be coming or going.

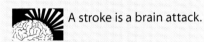 A stroke is a brain attack.

Another skill I miss was my ability to automatically sniff-out information in my short-term memory which doesn't need to be transferred to my long-term memory and purge it. I have a hunch lots of information which should have been purged has snuck into my long-term memory post-stroke.

Memories I don't *ask for* from decades ago surface a couple of times each week in what I call *Blasts from the Past*. Most of these memories are trivial, such as names of former pets or lines from old TV shows. Others are just plain funny, such as my tendency to blurt-out archaic words. These words are as foreign to today's generation as their lingo often is to me. For example, while complimenting a young woman about her hair, I asked what type of cream rinse she uses. "Cream rinse?" she questioned. When I said, "You know. The stuff you put on after shampooing to help keep your hair shiny." She said, "We call that conditioner."

And did you know the name of Baton Rouge, Louisiana, really should be Baton Blush to keep up with the times? I told my make-up saleslady I needed a new case of rouge and she burst into laughter. All I know is that when I took dance lessons as a little girl, Mom lathered my cheeks in **rouge**, not blush, before my performances.

My tendency to let long-term memories trump those filed more recently extends beyond simple words, too. One embarrassing example is remembering people and things as they were years ago rather than as they are now. When I got reconnected, via e-mail, with a college friend, I explained Troy's job based on work he'd been doing about eight years earlier, rather than his current position.

Most *Blasts from the Past* occur when I first wake-up, after a word or phrase has entered my mind while sleeping. Any day that starts with a *Blast* is going to be a good one, as far as I'm concerned. It's rather engaging to scan my long-term memory to figure out why I bothered to preserve these memories. My favorite one so far is the phrase *BR549*, mentioned earlier. Asking someone for help figuring out a *blast*, or turning to the Internet, is like giving up on a *Blast from the Past,* so I usually give myself overnight to think-on it before calling for back-up. The final step in my *Blast from the Past game* is to confirm my answer.

The first post office box I remember was unit #14, the box my parents rented until I was about eight. The combination to open #14 was H-F-DE. Perhaps I dialed it one too many times? When we upgraded to box #334, we got a new combination, but that one hasn't bubbled up yet.

Then there's the social security number of a young man I wrote to while he served in the Navy. He seemed more than a little surprised when I rattled-off that 9-digit number without a hitch over the phone, recently.

And would you believe my dad had a cat named Mademoiselle Hepzibah as a child? He mentioned her name to me in the early 1970s when I was trying to come-up with just the right name for my new cat.

> The address of my junior high pen pal occurred to me in a dream one night. When I awoke with an unusual address on my mind, I realized it might belong to my friend in Holland, whose name came to mind almost instantly. I recalled putting the first letter I'd gotten from her in my scrapbook, and located it in our basement. Naturally, I mailed a letter to her that day to tell my friend her address had survived my *severe insult to the brain.* Her response arrived back within about a week because she and her family had settled near her childhood home.

It can be tempting to dwell on the past, but there's nothing I can do to change history. With that reality in mind, I choose to focus on bringing glory to God with each step I take. That way, when I take my final step into Glory, I can lovingly tell my God, "Thank You, Father. I did the best I could with what you gave me. Mind if I ask You a few questions?"

James Thurber, writer and cartoonist, died of stroke complications at 66.

CHAPTER 15

SHE'S GOT A
WAY WITH WORDS

You're alive because God included you in His plans for this world. He also gave you the talents you'll need to fulfill His plan for you. Perhaps you're good with numbers or have outstanding athletic skills. Maybe you can teach anything—to anyone—or music may be your greatest strength.

God also gives some people the ability to influence others with words. These folks are born with the ability to communicate clearly, concisely, and in a compelling way. I'm one of those who got an extra helping of communication skills. Like all people, however, we communicators have free will, which means God doesn't dictate how we use our skills. I believe He expects all people, including communicators, to invest their skills glorifying Him.

That means I was way off track before my stroke because I was using my skills to build a lucrative career. Given my desire to outdo anyone who'd gone before me, I was climbing the corporate ladder rather quickly. One key connection—God—was

Gee, I wish... ...I'd gone skydiving. Now I have the saying, "the fall would be fun, but the landing's gotta hurt," stuck in my head.

missing from my life, however. Without His guidance, I was using my communications skills to achieve only worldly goals.

> Driving a car with a V8 engine resulted in me getting two speeding tickets soon after I got my driver's license. Dad was a bit surprised by them, saying, "I didn't think my daughter would turn-out to be the AJ Foyt of the family!"

Our Creator tells us in Joshua 22:5 to love and serve Him with all our heart and soul. It's pretty clear from this verse God expects us to focus our affection and attentions on Him. What remains a mystery to many folks is how God expects them to serve Him. It took more than 40 years for me to find-out what He has planned for my life.

The good news is that finding out how you can best serve God isn't a guessing game. All you need to do is ask, "What's next, Lord?" and wait patiently for His guidance. Then, after getting His answer, you find a way to refocus your life on serving God while honoring your earthly commitments. Before I began asking God that question, my priorities included:

- Excelling in an influential job;
- Building an adequate retirement nest egg;
- Achieving the highest education of anyone in my family; and
- Providing everything our family needed, plus some of what we wanted.

If these sound like your own priorities, I suggest you consider how these help you keep your affections set on things above, rather than things of this world. Rearranging your priorities may seem overwhelming at first but once you're saved and get into a constant conversation with God, I believe you'll feel pulled to invest your talents glorifying Him. If you heed that call, your focus will shift to glorifying God and your talents will be transformed into spiritual gifts. Constant conversation with God is commanded in 1 Thessalonians 5:17, which says, "Pray without ceasing."

I probably wouldn't have gotten around to asking, "What's next,

Lord?" if not for my stroke because I thought I had everything under control back then. There's just something about a close encounter with mortality that seems to help a person open her eyes to what's truly important. Perhaps my near-death experience supports the saying, "There are no atheists in fox holes or emergency rooms." Although I didn't doubt God's existence pre-stroke, I was disconnected from Him by sin because I hadn't accepted Jesus Christ as my Lord and Savior.

Stroke can affect a person's communication skills in a variety of ways, depending on the location and severity of the resulting brain injury. One common stroke deficit, aphasia, is the loss or impairment of the ability to use and understand words. Many stroke survivors—including me—face less obvious communication challenges. For example, it took several years for me to realize my stroke severely damaged my ability to <u>casually</u> participate in conversations and to read non-verbal cues.

If these communication losses were going to abate as my brain adjusted to its new organization, I figure I'd be back to *normal* by now. Given that I still feel their impact throughout each day, however, I assume they'll be with me the rest of my life. Overcoming cognitive challenges such as these requires self-discipline, and a willingness to try different approaches until I figure out what works for me.

Like the more tangible deficits mentioned earlier, learning to communicate clearly as an adult strikes me as more challenging than learning to a child. For example, how do people learn to stay on-topic? In some situations we're expected to stay focused on the subject at hand, while other times its okay to topic-hop. Most folks do seem to shift among topics which are somehow related, though. That restriction was lifted for me when I had my stroke. Now I have no qualms about going from Point A to Point N, with no stops in-between. This *tangentiality* (as the medical folks call it) seldom causes problems at home but was rather disruptive during my post-stroke time back at work.

Most folks also don't want to stick with the same topic for too long though or people may think they're weird. Remember that old saying about *beating a dead horse*? As a stroke survivor, I have a good reason for being unable to drop a topic and move on. That would be a cognitive challenge with the catchy name *perseveration*. Once you get me talking about something, my mouth starts spewing out information retrieved from the inner recesses of my brain and doesn't know when to stop. I've yet to find a way to prevent these humbling diatribes. Simply recognizing I suffer from perseveration doesn't help me shut-up at the right time.

My tendency to keep talking long after a topic is dead-and-gone is partially due to some organization issues in my brain. Before my stroke, I automatically recognized what information gathered through conversation was important and filed it in an organized way. Likewise, petty information was automatically purged. These days it's anyone's guess what information my brain will keep and what it'll toss. To complicate matters, what I do retain seems to be dumped into a *File Later* bucket. You know how well those slush piles work, right? Stuff goes in, the volume increases, and most things never surface again.

This change makes me think of the difference between using sand to build a castle versus tossing it into a sandbox. Both activities may include the same amount of sand but the end results are quite different. My brain has gathered a bunch of information provided in conversations since Jan. 30, 2000, but pulling that information together in response to a question is a real challenge. If a question calls on information stored in my long-term memory, however, I can generally respond pretty well.

One technique I've found for rebuilding my communication skills is to stay in constant conversation with God. It took a while to form this habit but it's automatic for me now. God knows every one of my thoughts anyway, even the ones I wish hadn't entered my mind, so why not turn them over to Him in prayer?

For example, you know those choice words you reserve for drivers who interfere with your progress on the road? These words are probably automatic for you and just slip-out at the *right* time. The driver you're cursing probably can't hear your comments, but God and anyone in your car certainly does. When you consider the fact

God hears everything you say, that's some good incentive to say, "Thank you, Father," when you narrowly avoid an accident.

If you feel the need to verbally respond to this type of encounter, why not say something that glorifies God? That comeback may sound corny as you read it here but will sound both wonderful and corny when you shout it at an offending driver. Besides, if there are children riding with you, they may well repeat what you said.

One observable benefit of my constant conversation with God is how it's polishing my interpersonal communication skills. Although I can say anything to God, in any way I want, I concentrate on sharing relevant information with Him in an appropriate way.

Chatting remains my greatest communication challenge. As my husband once said, "It's like you try to drive every conversation now." Troy was right about that and I'm grateful he pointed it out. Trying to dictate where our conversations went was my way of making our banter more predictable. I'm much more comfortable speaking when I've had a moment to arrange thoughts in my mind. However, by being too forward about setting the pace and direction of our conversations, I was causing them to be anything but casual.

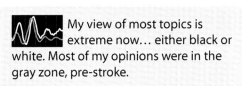 My view of most topics is extreme now… either black or white. Most of my opinions were in the gray zone, pre-stroke.

Out of respect for Troy's input, I now remind myself to *listen more and talk less* when someone strikes-up a conversation. If they started it, they should probably determine how it progresses. There may be some awkward pauses as I organize my thoughts but they do feel more casual. If I seem somewhat abrupt at times, that may be because I respond to questions as if I'm in a legal deposition, answering only the question asked and not volunteering information.

To further level the playing field, I do sometimes ask others to defer a conversation until they have my undivided attention. The grilled cheese sandwich experience mentioned earlier helped me realize multi-tasking isn't a good idea for me now. I'm also not shy about reminding folks, "I can only do 14 things at a time," my way of saying I feel overwhelmed and can't focus on what they're saying.

When I'm not sure if those I'm talking with are missing the point or zoning out, I ask one of my standard questions: "Enough said?" or "You know what I mean?" This gives them the chance to halt our conversation or ask me to restate a point. For questions that leave me in a state of shock, my first response is, "Tell me where you heard that." That's what Trent heard when he asked me about an infamous serial killer.

Written communication errors are easier for me to avoid because I know some trusted souls who provide input at different stages of my writing. However, no one provides input on what I say until after I speak. As a result, I often need to correct what I said so it accurately reflects what I think. Writing this book has been a blessing for me because it helped rebuild both my writing and conversation skills.

As with my more visible deficits, my conversation challenges get more severe if I'm under-the-weather, overly tired, or overwhelmed. They're also more noticeable in emotionally loaded situations and during conversations that move at an unpredictable pace. On the flip side, my stroke did eliminate my fear of public speaking. In fact, I'm now more comfortable addressing an audience than I am in casual conversation.

My ability to write and speak clearly is atypical for a stroke survivor, but quite different from what I could do before my stroke. Different doesn't always mean bad, though, now does it? As Pauline, one of my speech language pathologists, said, "E is the first stroke survivor I've worked with in more than 25 years who didn't lose the ability to anticipate what might confuse her audience."

That was quite a compliment but neither of us realized at the time how my stroke had rattled my ability to communicate clearly, appropriately, and concisely. Given that my stroke left me mute for *only* three days, you may be wondering why I even had speech therapy. As with every stroke deficit, the challenges a survivor faces are all about how well her brain does, or doesn't, communicate with various parts of her body.

In my case, my brain got back on speaking terms with my vocal system soon after my stroke, but the information rumbling around inside my skull often didn't come out quite right. Pauline was charged with helping me get these two systems back in sync so that what I was thinking about saying would come out of my mouth in a way others could understand, and only if it were appropriate for them to hear.

> **SideNote:** Relearning to speak (speech therapy) is linked with writing because before a person can speak intelligibly, he must organize thoughts in his mind. This is comparable to how writing is done except that speaking doesn't require paper and ink. By relearning to speak, I was also relearning to write. Clear communication requires both complex cognitive skills and experience. Although my stroke spared my years of communication experience, my cognitive skills took quite a hit.

Many folks would probably be grateful to have communication skills comparable to my post-stroke abilities, but golly I miss being able to automatically communicate in a way that positively impacts people. What I don't miss is the empty feeling I used to experience after writing about things of this world for my job in Corporate America. The beauty of my stroke is that it helped open my eyes to what I ought to be telling the world.

Most of my writing occurred automatically, before my stroke. Plans for how best to convey information to others just seemed to hit me back then, no matter how complex and/or mundane the topic. All of the information I absorbed about a topic seemed to congeal into a plan without deliberate attention from me.

My writing may have appeared impromptu to others because no one, including me, was aware of the behind-the-scenes work my brain had going on. It was using lots of energy, working through my innate communication processes. It's painfully obvious to me since my stroke that effective communication requires significant cognitive energy. Gone is the time when I could sit down and write a clear, concise, interesting message on-the-fly.

Words cannot express how grateful I am that I can think well enough to identify these processes. I recall being able to write well when tired, distracted, sick, and under great stress, before my stroke. Now I must be calm, well-rested, in good health, and have a clear focus to write well. How automatic does that sound?

Disciplining myself to follow these processes is an entirely different challenge. First I have to figure out how to get myself into the right frame-of-mind to apply them. It all starts with prayer, asking God to help me glorify His name as I write. Next, I remind myself that if the words I write bring glory to God, they'll be better than anything I ever wrote before.

When I want to write something these days, I coach myself to follow the processes I've identified and figure out how I can get my surviving brain cells lined-up well enough to work through them. These are the same communication processes my brain used to automatically apply to writing challenges. Identifying them has certainly been an eye-opening experience for me. This is where it's a good thing I have the rest of my life to get better, because training my mind to do what used to be an 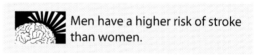 Men have a higher risk of stroke than women. innate ability is tiring and vexing.

If I forget to follow my processes, the words flow without ceasing, and without making a point. Worse yet, I tend to inadvertently say things that are hurtful and/or misleading. This happens more often with speaking than with writing. Since words can never be taken back, I frequently remind myself to think before speaking.

As mentioned earlier, I was born with strong communication skills and honed them through education and experience. These skills were transformed into spiritual gifts when I fully grasped that Jesus Christ died, was buried, and rose again so God would forgive my sins. (I Cor 15:1-4). This upgrade included a change in control over the thoughts rattling around inside my skull. Suddenly, the Holy Spirit, rather than my goals and desires, was guiding which thoughts my mind entertains. God's Holy Spirit immediately changed me forever and He began reaching out to others via my soul, mind, and body. Come to think of it, perhaps I should have used *He's* in this chapter title. After all, my words now stem from the Holy Spirit.

Recognizing my call shouldn't have been a surprise to me because I'd read Colossians 3:2 several times earlier in my life. That verse tells us to, "Set your affection on things above, not on things on the earth." That verse became meaningful to me when God's Holy Spirit took up residence in my soul.

That's how it is with most folks, isn't it? When things are going our way, we don't consider the possibility we may be following the wrong path. Then, we reach a fork in the road and comments which previously made no sense suddenly seem relevant. Like a light bulb above my head, that verse suddenly told me to glorify God with my communication abilities.

Minnie Pearl, another *Hee-Haw* star, died of stroke at 84.

CHAPTER 16

FREE FROM NOW
TO ETERNITY

This world would be a wonderful place if everyone were saved and kept their affection set on things above. Based on how people often treat one another, however, I'd say there are lots of folks who've yet to accept the truth of Jesus Christ's sacrifice, and be born again.

Perhaps that's why Jesus' words in Matthew 6:26-34 seem so challenging. These verses tell me I shouldn't worry about **anything**. They also remind me that God provides food for the birds He created, and beautifully clothes His flowers. Jesus then tells me God values human life more highly than these other creations. I take that to mean God will provide for us — His most favored creation even more readily than He does for His animals and plants.

The clincher comes in verse 33, which says, "But seek ye first the kingdom of God, and his righteousness; and all these things shall be added unto you." This verse tells me God will meet the needs of those who keep Him as their top priority. Earlier in my spiritual journey, I

Gee,
I wish...
...I'd learned
to snow ski.

didn't take that verse so literally. Now it tells me, quite clearly, to focus on God and have faith He'll provide what I need.

In verse 34, I hear Jesus encouraging me to focus only on today's challenges and think about tomorrow when it gets here. That can be a tall order when I hear others fretting about college expenses and retirement needs, but it makes sense. Many folks I know spend a lot of time and energy *what-iffing* (AKA worrying about what might happen).

God has led me to believe the concept of focusing only on today also applies to the breadth of information I should heed. When Jesus says to focus on today's challenges, I think He means I should focus on the challenges *at-hand*. This world is full of interesting information, available 24/7, but most of it has nothing to do with me or my relationship with Jesus Christ. That's one reason I stopped following the news years ago.

Knowing God will meet my needs doesn't mean He magically keeps our pantry and refrigerator stocked. He also doesn't keep the gas tank in my car full. As I said earlier, God doesn't micromanage this world. He created us with free will and is letting us find our own way. He does, however, help every saved person meet her own needs.

Here's a quick look at how He helps me:

1. God knows what I **need** and **want** better than I could ever articulate.
2. He waits for me to submit my needs and wants to Him in prayer. When I pray, I thank God for what He's already provided, tell Him what I need/want, and ask what my next move should be.
3. Waiting patiently for God's response is an interesting challenge for me but when His guidance arrives, it comes in a form that works really well for me, yet is invisible to others.
4. After learning what my next step should be, I tell myself to use all of the skills He gave me to take it, and ask Him to handle what's beyond my control.

When handing the *uncontrollables* over to Him, I also commit to not worry about them.

5. Only then do I take my next step.

Example: I offered several publishers the chance to print this book. After developing a book proposal, I mailed query letters to them and asked God to prompt the right one to respond. A few asked to see my book proposal, but none accepted it. Dejected, I asked God what step I should take next and He led me to *LuLu.com*. After getting familiar with the site, I asked Him how anyone would discover *Praise God* if I went with that option. He immediately let me know He'd take care of promotion and marketing. God reminds me periodically that my role is to tell my story; He'll ensure it falls into the hands of the right readers.

I now take a similar approach with each want and need, which means I no longer have any worries. Ridding my life of worry is the greatest blessing of being born again that I can have in this world. I didn't realize God would do that for me until I was saved. Entering into eternity with God when I die is the best blessing of all.

Our Creator offers each person the chance to wipe the stain of sin from his life. That opportunity is free, open to everyone, attainable, carries eternal significance, and provides immediate benefits to each recipient. Isn't that just like God? Accepting His Grace is significant, yet simple, and, no one can accept His Grace for someone else. Sounds kind of like falling in love, doesn't it?

It's wonderful to be free of all the stress and worries I carted around for almost four decades. My words can't do justice to how wonderful this freedom feels but John 10:10 says, Jesus came to give us *abundant life*. Suffice it to say, my life with Jesus Christ enables me to relax, make wise decisions, and feel less anxious, even when times get tough. As an added bonus, I can see God's glory in every situation.

God is everywhere, all the time, so His glory is (obviously) everywhere, too. Walking through this life with the light of Jesus Christ in my heart, I can find God's glory in any situation, regardless of how bad it appears. I now stay in constant conversation with God, too, particularly when the going gets tough.

When something bad happens in life, which happens to every-one occasionally, it can be tempting to ask, "Why me?" or say, "That's not fair." When those moments arise in my life, I keep viewing the situation from different angles, with an open mind and open heart, until I *find God* in it.

By following in Jesus' footsteps, I can overcome any temptation Satan casts my way. Since love for Christ overtook my life, I live for Him, rather than myself. When I wholeheartedly accepted the truth of His sacrifice, I was permanently freed from the bondage of any sin I'd ever committed or might commit in the future. It's so amazing to be completely free when I awaken each morning—the weight of the world is no longer on my shoulders.

As an added bonus, I no longer fear death, not that I'm in any hurry to reach that milestone. Medical folks may find ways to pre-vent and cure more diseases almost daily, but their efforts won't make any of us immortal. No amount of knowledge will protect people from war, starvation, and violence. These atrocities are ex-amples of the end result of sins such as anger, desire, greed, jeal-ousy, laziness, and pride.

God created humans as mortal beings, according to Genesis 3:19. This verse says, "In the sweat of thy face shalt thou eat bread, till thou return unto the ground; for out of it wast thou taken: for dust thou art, and unto dust shalt thou return." Perhaps this verse is the source of the old *dust-to-dust* line used at many celebrations of life (AKA funerals)?

 Heredity plays a role in the risk of ischemic, but not hemorrhagic, stroke.

Like most folks, I *got the message* I'm mortal when I was about 12. The full concept of mortality didn't register until a good friend of mine, Lee, died about a year out of high school, though. The real *kicker* came a few years post-stroke when I realized mortality even applies to me. There's nothing like a mind-altering, near-death ex-perience for driving that point home. How wonderful I also came to know I need not fear death. It will simply mark the beginning of a new reality for me because Jesus Christ is my Lord and Savior.

Being one step away from Glory—eternity with God in

Heaven — prompted me to start saying, "Things always work out," a few years back. I repeat that phrase to myself, Troy, the boys, and select others when things don't seem to be going our way. After all, each event in a person's life is one tiny piece of God's master plan and those pieces will eventually all fit together, bringing His plan to fruition.

That notion reminds me of the beautiful, patchwork quilts my grandma used to craft. Grandma E saved every scrap of cloth she could during the Great Depression to make quilts for her family. None of those scraps was worth anything on their own, but under her mastery they became functional works of art. I think the same is true of spiritual gifts. 1 Corinthians 12:4 tells us, "There are diversities of gifts, but the same Spirit."

Each person contributes a piece to God's big plan/quilt, which becomes more complete when someone else steps up to fulfill his role. The spiritual gifts of each Christian wouldn't amount to much on their own but when united and focused on glorifying God, they can change the world. If you're unsure where your piece goes, all you need to do is ask God. He's the One who knows how everything fits together.

It's such a comfort knowing God's plan includes every detail about each person's life, beginning before conception and ending with death. Although He knows everything that will happen to each person, He doesn't force any worldly event to happen.

Now that I'm saved, my priorities are: God, family, and others. It's such a blessing to finally feel complete and know my priorities are godly. They're also easy to remember and explain to others. Sometimes I have to remind Troy, Trent, and Don they take second place to God but who can feel too badly about that?

Those intent on banishing God from public schools and other government institutions sometimes extract text from the First Amendment to the Constitution of the United States of America to make their case. The **full** text of that amendment came to me in a Blast from the Past. If it's been awhile since you read the First Amendment, here it is (emphasis mine):

Congress shall make no law respecting an establishment **of religion,** or **prohibiting the free exercise thereof;** or abridging the freedom of speech, or of the press; or the right of the people peaceably to assemble, and to petition the Government for a redress of grievances.

Making a living used to be my top priority and now it doesn't even make the list. That's because I now know things always work out. Although I don't control much in this world, I do control how much I let this world affect my relationship with God, my loved ones, and with others, when I rely on His Guidance.

It's a good thing my focus is now clear because Satan would probably have really appreciated it if I'd kept my spiritual beliefs to myself. He subjected me to countless temptations while writing this book, doing his best to throw me off-track.

Having my mind forcibly detached from worldly cares, allowed me to relax long enough to let God's love infuse my heart. Knowing my soul now has a reserved spot in Heaven provides total freedom from the cares of this world, leaving me free to make the most of each day. Jesus' parable of the lamp (told in Matthew 5:15, Mark 4:21, and Luke 11:33) helps explain this change in my communication focus.

This parable tells me that when God equips someone with a talent, she should use it to share His love with others. She shouldn't keep her skills hidden away, like a light under a basket. Rather, she should display her talent like a light on a candlestick.

To me, focusing my communication skills on achieving material gains was like hiding them under a basket. That approach helped me succeed in Corporate America for many years, until my stroke. Early in my recovery, I tried to reclaim my pre-stroke role in the world. In fact, it took more than six years for me to figure out why I'd lost interest in this world and shifted my focus to God.

That reality sunk-in one evening while studying the book of Matthew with some church friends. That's when the Holy Spirit helped me see my life experiences were coming together in a way I can use to bring Glory to God. You can only imagine how overwhelming it was to hear myself tell my friends, "My stroke is the best thing that's ever happened to me."

That statement is entirely true because until my stroke, I (mistakenly) thought I had everything under control. In retrospect, I think Satan was using control as a temptation to keep me from getting to know Jesus Christ.

Although my stroke is the biggest, ugliest challenge I've faced, it happened at just the right time. It took a severe brain injury and about 40 years for me to realize what Jesus Christ means to me. When I finally *got it*, it was as if Someone had lifted the weight of the world from my shoulders. It was amazing to realize that spending eternity with God depended only on me relinquishing control over my life. Talk about the mother of all mind-benders…

When my love for Christ merged with my life experiences and talents, my role as a story-teller surfaced

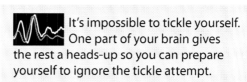

It's impossible to tickle yourself. One part of your brain gives the rest a heads-up so you can prepare yourself to ignore the tickle attempt.

and my attention shifted from the materialistic goals mentioned earlier to glorifying God. My mind stays clear now because no human is driving my thoughts. I believe I write better now than ever before because I now have a message others <u>need</u> to hear. What I used to write about was important in this world, but not beyond.

Before I was saved, I didn't know every human **needs** God to beat Satan. Our free will makes us susceptible to temptation and the only way we can consistently resist it is with the Holy Spirit's guidance. To grasp this concept, you might picture yourself as the flag tied at the middle of a tug-of-war rope. One team is standing in Heaven, encouraging you to step in. The other is pulling you toward hell.

The Heaven Team represents guidance provided by the Holy Spirit. After you accept Jesus Christ as your Lord and Savior, God will answer every question you ask Him.

Team hell represents temptations Satan casts our way. He regularly sets opportunities to sin in front of every person, both those who are saved and those yet-to-be-saved. I struggled for a while with why Satan bothers to tempt saved people. After all, he can't win-over the soul of someone who's truly accepted Jesus Christ as his Lord and Savior. When I finally found the answer, it was **so** obvious. Satan probably does that because getting a saved person to succumb to temptation may push those yet-to-be-saved further away from God, if they see his *fall*.

Although I stay in constant conversation with God now, I still fall for one of Satan's temptations now-and-then. That's because God doesn't **force** me to do as He suggests. In fact, God doesn't **make** anyone do anything. The old saying, "The devil made me do it," is equally inaccurate. Neither God nor Satan can make a person do anything, because we have free will.

Regardless of how God answers my prayers, our conversations are strictly between Him and me. I appreciate this *confidentiality* but it can get tricky if God guides me to do something that catches a loved one off-guard. I've learned through experience it's sometimes best to find a way to explain my actions which doesn't involve openly saying, "God told me to do it."

It's a good thing my new priorities keep me from *what-iffing* because I think Satan can use *what-ifs* to distract a saved person from glorifying God. My response to most "What if…" questions is to turn them around by saying, "What if we make the most of today and worry about that **if** we need to?" For example, if the concern is, "What if it becomes a crime to say 'One nation under God' in a public school?" I may say, "What if every person in our public schools stayed in constant, silent conversation with God?"

Bringing glory to God wasn't on my pre-stroke to-do list, and knowing me, I wouldn't have willingly taken a break from my driven life to make it one. I was too busy running the rat race.

God knew every thought I entertained and saw every move I made during my first 40 years but had no input on my decisions. How could He? God doesn't force Himself on anyone and I hadn't yet come to know Jesus Christ died so my sins could be forgiven. God remained available to me all that time, ready to share His love with me when I accepted the Saving Grace provided by His Son.

If you're not yet saved, what's the hold-up? You have only this lifetime to get reconnected with God. Fortunately, I wasted *only* about 40 years before tuning into what the Holy Spirit has to tell me. Now I have the rest of my life to become as much like Jesus Christ as possible. Sure, He's the only perfect human who's ever lived but why set my sights on anything short of perfection?

God longs to be in fellowship with each human being but is simply an onlooker until a person cleanses his life of sin. The only way to remove that stain from your life is to accept the atonement provided by Jesus' sacrificial death. The bottom line is that when you die, your soul will *relocate* either to Heaven (united with God) or to hell (separated from God) for the remainder of eternity. If you think it's tough to get out of a lease down here, there's no option in eternity. Your final destination is set forever when you die.

Having a massive stroke could easily have been the end of me. Sustaining a brain injury in my right hemisphere could have left me unable to think of anything to say. What a blessing it *blotted-out* the static in my life so I could finally relax enough to reach-out to God. The impact of His presence in the early years of my recovery first changed my heart, and then changed my mind. One result of these changes is that I now seem able to write well **only** about topics that are near-and-dear to my heart.

When you get reconnected with God, I believe you'll find more joy in your life, too. True freedom in this world starts with God. He's the only One who can provide the freedom each of us needs to become the person He created.

The most important thing for you to know about sin is that Jesus Christ is the only One who can wipe its stain from your life. He'll do that for you when you come to believe He died on the Cross in atonement for your sins and was resurrected three days later to sit at the right hand of God. Why wait for a near-death experience to get your life in order?

ee cummings, American poet, died of stroke at 67.

Where Will You
Spend Eternity?

God created people in His own image from the dust of the ground. He made the first person, Adam, a *living soul* by breathing the breath of life into his nostrils (Genesis 2:7). That first soul probably sensed God's presence even before God spoke to Adam in the Garden of Eden.

Adam's descendents—every person in this world—are linked to God by that original life-giving breath. As a result, each of us has a *living soul* which prompts us to feel incomplete until we're in relationship with God. The catch is that, "…all have sinned, and come short of the glory of God" (Romans 3:23). This verse tells me that every person is separated from God by sin at birth, by default.

A newborn baby hasn't committed a sin, obviously, but she's born with what I think of as a *sin connection*. This permanent connection between humanity and Satan exists because Eve, then Adam, ate the one fruit in the Garden of Eden that God told them to leave alone. Their decision to disobey God gave Satan the opportunity to establish his *sin connection*.

Your *sin connection*, like your living soul, was present at birth and will never go away. Their purposes are also similar: to influence where your soul will spend eternity. The key difference is that God's breath (your living soul) encourages you to rid your life of sin and be in relationship with God so your soul will spend eternity in Heaven when you physically die. The enemy uses your *sin connection* to tempt you to sin and to keep you distant from God so your soul will spend eternity in hell after you die.

Many people mistakenly believe they can overcome the enemy's temptations on their own and perform *good enough* to get into Heaven. These folks seem to think God will cut them some slack, when the time comes, if they've done more *good* than *evil* during their lifetime.

Several popular religions are even based on that **errant** notion. God addresses such distractions in **Proverbs 14:12** saying, "There is a way which seemeth right unto a man, but the end thereof are the ways of death." A more direct statement comes in **Romans 3:4** which says, "God forbid: yea, let God be true, but every man a liar…"

Nowhere in the Holy Bible does God say that He's keeping track of all your good works and your sins so He can let you know if you're *good enough* for admission when you reach the gates of Heaven. Our Heavenly Father does tell us, "For the wages of sin is death; but the gift of God is eternal life through Jesus Christ our Lord." (Romans 6:23) This verse refers to spiritual—rather than physical—death, of course. Every human body will one day die but you get to choose whether your soul lives forever in Heaven or dies an eternal death in hell.

You'll need to read and study God's Word in the Holy Bible on your own to figure out if you're ready to be saved, but here are a few verses that led me to accept Jesus Christ as my Lord and Savior:

- For by grace are ye saved through faith; and that not of yourselves: it is the gift of God: Not of works, lest any man should boast. *(Ephesians 2:8-9)*
- For the preaching of the cross is to them that perish foolishness; but unto us which are saved it is the power of God. *(1 Corinthians 1:18)*
- He that findeth his life shall lose it: and he that loseth his life for my sake shall find it. *(Matthew 10:39)*
- For there is one God, and one mediator between God and men, the man Christ Jesus. *(1 Timothy 2:5)*
- For Christ also hath once suffered for sins, the just for the unjust, that he might bring us to God, being put to death in the flesh, but quickened by the Spirit. *(1 Peter 3:18)*

Okay. So if you're not yet saved, you have some thinking to do before you die. No amount of knowledge or medical advancements will make you immortal but God's love and the Saving Grace available through our Lord Jesus Christ provide a way for you to live forever, if **you choose** to be saved.

My prayer is that reading *Praise God for Tattered Dreams* has helped you see how personal tragedy can prompt wonderful change. If you're still stumblin' through this life without God's Holy Spirit guiding you, you need only accept the sacrifice Jesus Christ made on your behalf some 2,000 years ago. When you believe **in your heart** that Jesus died in your place and was resurrected by God—so God will forgive your sins—you'll know physical death is just a bump in the road for a saved person.

God made only one of you and He has a plan for your life. Your job is to figure out what purpose He created you to fill, and then to fulfill it. You'll need His Holy Spirit walking with you in this lifetime to *get 'er done.*

Jesus did everything He could for you on the Cross of Calvary. If you've yet to accept His Gift of love, isn't it time for you to take that leap of faith? There's really no reason for you to stumble through life disconnected from God by sin.

After you're saved, I think you'll find more joy in your life than you ever imagined possible. Better yet, you'll know death is simply a rite of passage between this world and into the presence of God in Heaven.

APPRECIATION

Several friends I've gathered along my life's journey helped create this book. They're *misnamed* below because any glory associated with *Praise God for Tattered Dreams* should go to God, not them. Hopefully, each will recognize the pseudonym I chose for them.

To God be the Glory,
E.

Known as...	How contributed	Known E. since
A - I - E	Editing, spiritual insight	1987
Dorie	Encouragement, spiritual insight	2003
DClink	Organization, editing	1992
MySLP	Spiritual insight, editing	2003
JE5	Encouragement, spiritual insight	1986
MiPS	Editing, file recovery	1992
Mr. BG	Design, editing	1982
PixBugg	Editing, encouragement	2001
Gr8barista	Editing, encouragement	2007
Lilly's mom	Organization and encouragement	1992
Lesler	Encouragement, editing	2009